D1070470

CONTEMPORARY ESSAYS
1933

CONTEMPORARY ESSAYS
1933

EDITED
WITH AN INTRODUCTION
BY
SYLVA NORMAN

Essay Index Reprint Series

 BOOKS FOR LIBRARIES PRESS
FREEPORT, NEW YORK

First Published 1933
Reprinted 1968

LIBRARY OF CONGRESS CATALOG CARD NUMBER:
68-29235

PRINTED IN THE UNITED STATES OF AMERICA

CONTENTS

INTRODUCTION   SYLVA NORMAN   vii

THE COUNTRY

The Last Squire   ADRIAN BELL   3
Return in Winter   KATE O'BRIEN   19
The Earth Being Troubled   PHILIP TOMLINSON   33

BOOKS AND AUTHORS

Footnote to Lawrence   RICHARD GOODMAN   51
Henry James—An Aspect   GRAHAM GREENE   65
Anger Against Books   NAOMI MITCHISON   77

THE VISIONARY GLEAM

Spirit of Death   TANGYE LEAN   97
The Triumph of Time   JAMES LAVER   113
Sable Goddess   DEREK HUDSON   139
Gubbins on Love   MICHAEL ROBERTS   151

SKETCHES FROM EXPERIENCE

The Returned Traveller   PETER FLEMING   175
Fall In, Ghosts   EDMUND BLUNDEN   187

INTRODUCTION

INTRODUCTION

I

"THERE are two sorts of writing", Hazlitt remarks in his
Table Talk. The first, he explains, is compilation, and aims
at enlightening the reader on all that is known already of a
question. "An author of this class is a very learned amanu-
ensis of other people's thoughts." The second sort of writing
assumes the reader to have a general knowledge of the subject,
and proceeds to fill up blanks and explore new pathways in a
disjointed but adventurous way. It is thus "a set of additions
and corrections to other men's works, or to the common stock
of human knowledge, printed separately".

Whether or not such a division controls the whole ground
of literature, it does apply to the editing of books. There are
two sorts of editing, and Hazlitt's definition can be adapted to
them. The first consists in presenting already existent matter,
whether by tearing scraps from their various former settings
to make a pattern in a new scheme (as *Great Sea Stories of
All Nations*, or *A Dog-Lover's Anthology*) or by serving up a
single piece of work with relevant comments. An editor of this
type is at best a scholar and classicist, at worst an appreciator
of good work. The explorative editor begins with nothing more
tangible than an idea of how he may encourage new ten-
dencies; he then looks for a sympathetic and sporting publisher
who will back up the experiment. This type of editor is not
necessarily an iconoclast or a rebel; he is a creature who has
hope and curiosity, and proposes to test them.

In this figure of the explorative editor is the explanation of
a book of heterogeneous new essays, where you may search
vainly for a common theme, a logical sequence, or a close link
between one writer and another. For the intention is not to
limit the field but rather to extend it, and my rough grouping

of these essays does not proceed from any pre-arranged plan. It is attempted for convenience only. Without it they might look like those random dots on a blank sheet of paper that were a test of ingenuity in my nursery days. "Draw a motor-car, an elephant or an apple tree, keeping your pencil on the paper, and taking care to go through every dot." The ingenious may still have a try at it. No doubt a motor-car, an elephant or an apple tree could yet be constructed out of this collection, if we take them to mean movement, strength and fruitfulness. But since I am not seeking or expecting a closed outline we may leave this puzzle unsolved. The essay lends itself all too easily, as a rule, to a particular classification. We need only open at random any present-day author's collected pieces to find that they are a garner of reprinted newspaper articles: leaders, back-pagers, or the middles that act as buffers between politics and book-reviews in a weekly journal. There is nothing unpleasing about such articles, and nothing offensive; the editor of the paper, to be sure, must see to that. In addition, he prefers them to be topical. For instance, a hurried reader will be caught by an article on convicts if a notable criminal escaped two days before; if not, an article on convicts becomes academic when thrust between a discussion of war debts and a column on Mr Z's gigantic new novel. You cannot be highly personal, meditative or irrelevant in a middle article; you must not be too startling, and again you cannot well afford the still small voice. For, as contributor to a periodical, you are part of a team, and although your own first business might seem to be to communicate your sincere thoughts on a subject, the editor's first business is to see that his paper holds together, without violent dissonances of matter or style.

Apart from these carefully trimmed models of conformity there is little enough scope for exercise of the essay form. Any reflections that a writer has to offer nowadays must be put into the guise of fiction if he intends them to have hearers. We might perhaps go so far back as to blame Fielding for originating this essay-in-the-novel plan, were it not that the case was almost reversed in his day. Fiction was the new departure, and one may guess that a public used to *Spectators*, *Tatlers* and *Guardians* found no difficulty in relishing the essays interspersed in *Tom Jones*. When they reached them they were on known territory. But what has happened to that territory? The sea of fiction has almost washed over its surface, and we appear to have been glad enough, since we have learnt to swim about and now find that strolling on an island is a slow pedestrian job—exhausting even. So our new habits are losing us the essay, and a once fertile land of prose is left uncultivated and partially submerged.

There appears to be some reason for reclaiming it. The essay has been so universal and so flexible a form that we must believe it will go on altering and developing if we allow it a reasonable chance. The only way to allow it one (since only fiction and biography have safe rewards at present) is to give authors some faint inducement to write essays in a manner that appeals to them and on a subject dictated by their own fancy rather than by the accident of events. This is my plan—or lack of plan, if you prefer to call it so—in the present volume. Each contributor was asked to choose his or her own subject with complete freedom, and if the result appears at first sight to be an untameable diversity I shall defend it by borrowing Hazlitt's words: "It is vain to object to this last style that it is disjointed, disproportioned, and irregular". And actually I believe that none of these sins so dominates as to counteract the advantages of an open field.

In suggesting this, I am far from claiming that no other chances for essayists, beyond what these pages afford, are to be found in London. Various pamphlet series have existed and continue to exist, although my own experience in attempting to edit essays in this form has convinced me that the authors thereby lose about nine-tenths of their potential readers. Pamphlets are not obtainable from circulating libraries, and they are rarely enough obtainable from book-

sellers, who, being concerned not only with reading matter but
with a spruce shop window, have a general horror of the dust-
collecting properties of paper booklets. Pamphlets are too expensive from the buyer's point of view and too cheap from the
seller's; so that before their contents ever come to be discussed
they have been rejected and condemned by both parties.
Stories, we are told, might just get by in sixteen pages octavo
and a wrapper, but essays never. There is almost a groan at
mention of them, such is the force of prejudice that has intervened between us and our chances of enjoyment.

II

Perhaps school-days are to blame for our modern repugnance
even to Elia and Macaulay. *Write an essay on Dash or Blank or
What not, paying special attention to your handwriting, your grammar
and your spelling, and remembering that marks are given for Style.*
Two hours for the paper, and the essay is Question 4. It is not
good enough, nor is the essay when we have scribbled it, with
the anticipatory echo in our ears of a "dreadful bell" or a
harsh order to collect the papers. This tyranny undoubtedly
has its use as journalistic training. Clamorous printers, press-
day, "proofs—immediate", are well enough served by that
earlier discipline. But our longer essay depends ultimately on
keeping clear of it (and I here apologise to those of my con-
tributors who have had to move within a time limit, but whose
work bears no trace of my hustling). By a longer essay I mean
not merely length in words but length in rhythm, in thought
and in tune. It is a length that includes depth and richness;
it may even, by its music, satisfy Sir Thomas Browne as "a
sensible fit of that harmony which intellectually sounds in the
ears of God". The essayist, at least, should not live in mental
disputation. He should be reconciled preferably to life and
certainly to himself. So finally, at the opposite pole from the
schoolboy effort (and let us skirt warily round the Prize Essay
with its courageous flounderings in a noble bog), we have the

ordered meditations on our universe that are granted to a mind serene and leisured.

It is even possible to carry this intellectual finality too far. Some minds—and Browne's may be included amongst them —appear to have matured in darkness. They accept the scheme of things with such resignation that the colour and diversity of life are lost to them. When Browne says, "I am of a constitution so general, that it consorts and sympathiseth with all things", we may bless his toleration, but we feel suspicious. And our suspicions are at once justified when he goes on, "I wonder not at the French for their dishes of Frogs, Snails and Toadstools, nor at the Jews for Locusts and Grasshoppers". So much the worse for Sir Thomas as an essayist, for unless we can wonder at the sweet absurdity of preferences we shall never write a Dissertation on Roast Pig. Infinite tolerance becomes a gloomy matter; it rounds off activity so completely that our ultimate pronouncement is an ode to death, and we are left groping, with Browne's predecessor, Drummond of Hawthornden, within the reverential dignity of a cypress grove. It is most impressive—for ten minutes on a bus-top—to read Drummond. He has resolved all discords, wiped out petty pleasures, ambitions, annoyances, and given us a god's or a Spengler's sense of cycles and mortality in which, not ripeness, but the going hence, is all.

The ghastly wonders of the world, raised by the ambition of ages, are overthrown and trampled: some lights above, not idly entitled stars, are lost, and never more seen of us: the excellent fabric of this universe it self, [do we hear an echo of Prospero?] shall one day suffer ruin, or a change like a ruin; and should poor earthlings thus to be handled complain?

And further:

Dost thou think thou leavest life too soon? Death is best young. Things fair and excellent, are not of long endurance upon earth. Who liveth well liveth long.

Resignation and serenity can go no further. But meanwhile our bus has reached Oxford Circus and we get out and cross

it with the usual attention to oncoming traffic. Drummond
has not helped our crossing or altered our convictions, for he
is writing at some millions of miles from Oxford Circus, and
indulging a remote astronomical vision of the world. "Who
can be great on so small a round as is this earth, and bounded
with so short a course of time?" And later in the essay he is
at some pains to prove (in 1623—ten years before Galileo's
better-known recantation) that the globe of the earth is but
as a point, since the stars appear of a like greatness from both
valleys and mountains, and to every part the heaven shows
"the half of its inside".

And so it may be, but the matter is relative. A philosophy of
earth worked out, as it were, in interplanetary space tends
naturally to ignore man's presence except as a small regular
growth akin to vegetables, and his motions, except in broadest
outlines, as a rising and setting comparable to the sun's. As
long as we take this view we may say it is not possible to be
completely reconciled to life while we dispute death as the
aim of all our movements. But we are not living on those
cosmic heights, and from our earthly view-point Browne and
more especially Drummond seem not to be floating in the
divine ether so much as to be standing with a foot in the grave.
Heaven perhaps knows what they have gained. The rest of us
are keenly conscious of their losses. They are without zest and
humanity and personal prejudice, they lack the excellent vices
of curiosity and attention to trifles (unless these are fictitious
trifles such as Browne's elaborate inquiry into the phoenix
and griffin), and, bestowing all their cadences on burial urns,
mortality and godhead, have not a tune left that a man may
dance a jig to and feel himself a lucky fellow to be alive.

This is not the attitude of the born essayist. Let us turn to
Lamb, and see what reflections about death and eternity
occur to him on New Year's Eve (remembering, however,
that Drummond of Hawthornden was to him one of "the
sweetest names, and which carry a perfume in the mention").
Lamb writes:

I care not to be carried with the tide, that smoothly bears human life to eternity; and reluct at the inevitable course of destiny. I am in love with this green earth; the face of town and country; the unspeakable rural solitudes, and the sweet security of streets....I do not want to be weaned by age; or drop, like mellow fruit, as they say, into the grave.

The protest continues, the list of earth's bounties and delights stretches out, until we join heartily with the author in drowning the foul phantom death and its impertinence in another cup of the generous.

We are at home here. Lamb—or Elia, not the brother of mad Mary—has a comfortable footing on the earth, and so we can read his essays while lolling in an arm-chair with a cigarette or stretched in the lee of a gorse bush on the Downs. To me a transcendental essayist is a far odder fish than an infidel astronomer. As a genuine essayist, we cannot find that he exists at all. It may be held that no matter what lesser men may do, when a French seigneur of the sixteenth century retires to a high tower in Perigord he should contemplate the stars out of his window and philosophise on them. But Seigneur Michel de Montaigne, having a room full of books and a mind given to curious observation rather than systems of study, remains genially present, showing us by precept and example what a blessing it can be to relish life and literature in a random fashion, and discreetly substitute one's personality ("myself am the groundworke of my booke") for the knowledge of experts. He repeatedly expounds his method of procedure—modestly, and almost in the guise of an attack on himself:

He that shall make search after knowledge, let him seek it where it is: there is nothing I professe lesse. These are but my fantasies by which I endevour not to make things known, but my selfe.

Later we have a frank, half-proud, and half-contemptuous avowal:

This hudling up of so much trash, or packing of so many severall pieces, is done so strangely, as I never lay hands on it but when an over lazie idlenesse urgeth me, and nowhere but in mine owne house. So has it beene compact at sundry pauses, and contrived at severall intervals.... My purpose is to represent the progress of my humours, that every part be seen or member distinguished as it was produced.

To be personal and not obtrusive, familiar and not petty, learned and not professorial, contrary and not crabbed: these are some of the virtues of your true essayist. He should not be over-ambitious of knowledge or perfection, or those sterner aims will cramp his blitheness; his ideas will crystallise and cease to flow. It is a common thing in the present day as in earlier centuries for a gifted writer to groan over his lack of expert knowledge on any subject, or to be so acutely conscious of the good writing that preceded him as to be discouraged from his own efforts. I should describe such a writer as having the meat of his discourse ready to hand, but lacking the juice to stew it in. So it is either thrown away or served up in hard pellets as maxims. There are two notable examples of this quandary in France. The first is La Bruyère, who deplores, "All is said, and one comes too late, now that there have been men for seven thousand years, and men, too, that have thought". A century later Joubert, who tormented himself by some inner necessity of putting "a whole book into a page, a whole page into a phrase, and that phrase into a word", cries out, "All the things which are easy to say well have been perfectly said; the rest is our business or our task: painful task!"

It is not surprising that Joubert and La Bruyère were driven to write maxims. Anything more diffuse would have seemed in their eyes a waste of paper, for it could never occur to them that an easier elasticity would make their painful task a happier one to themselves and their readers. The "all-is-said" attitude belongs to those with too stern a judgment of their work. They write slowly and reluctantly, searching every sentence for a phrase they can tighten and a word they can lop off, until, in passages massed with clotted thought, the jewel they would give to us is in a ten times barred-up chest, and few readers have either time or patience to pick the padlocks. Montaigne is not among those few. "If in reading", he says, "I fortune

to meet with any difficult points, I fret not my selfe about
them, but after I have given them a charge or two, I leave
them as I found them. Should I earnestly plod upon them,
I should loose both time and my selfe, for I have a skipping
wit.... I doe nothing without blithenesse."

I doe nothing without blithenesse might be taken as a motto
for the discursive essayist. It is far from implying archness,
superficiality or facetiousness in the resultant essay. What it
indicates is enjoyment in the writer, and the feeling, not of
mental strain, but of a mental holiday that will allow him to
roam, free of all legalised procedure, over his book-shelves and
through his meadows, collecting an odd volume or a meditative comment as he pleases. Whether the subject that comes
up be "vain and idle" or "noble and out-worne", he neither
rejects it nor exhausts it. There are a thousand ways of dealing
with every subject, and each particular way may seem to be
the best. It is not even strictly necessary to be burdened with
an opinion if curious matter and a graceful manner will play
substitute. As an example, take Montaigne's discourse (just
before "Cowardice the Mother of Cruelty") upon "Thumbs".
The subject strikes us as unpromising. Had not Slawkenbergius
on Noses a more genial task? However, Montaigne dips into
the classics (as usual), and finds a report that barbarous kings
would tie two thumbs together to confirm a covenant, wringing them till the blood came and then pricking them. Without
commenting on such behaviour (condemnation is reserved
for the next essay) he passes to further curious facts without
the sting. In Rome it was a sign of favour to kiss the thumbs
and of disfavour or disgrace to turn them outward. An echo
unborn when Montaigne wrote sounds in the reader's ears
immediately:

"I will bite my thumb at them; which is a disgrace to them, if
they bear it."
"Do you bite your thumb at us, sir?"
"I do bite my thumb, sir."

But the next paragraph tells us that "Lacedaemon masters

punished their schollers by byting their thumbs". Had Shakespeare read his Montaigne and misremembered him? —As for this cruelty of wringing thumbs, it might become a kindness. (This is my own deduction, not the essayist's.) A maimed thumb meant dispensation from going to war, since weapons could not be gripped without a thumb. And a Roman knight was punished for cutting off the thumbs of two young children to prevent their going. In our day we can appreciate this cruel mercy, for we almost remember how the amputation of a leg spelled home and could be welcomed. No reasonable father amputates his son's leg as a precaution, but a thumb is a less essential member, and the certainty of this small maiming might well be chosen against the odds of a great one.

So we may go on meditating over Montaigne's tune, which has all been sung in a bare three hundred words. Few of us can put so much potential thought so casually into a brief passage; nor can we complain (although it has been said of Montaigne) that the matter is packed too closely to be read with comfort. His commentary on life is quiet and natural as moss on a stone wall. It grows close, covering all crudities with its friendly furriness, and instead of being laid out formally it spreads, so that we have anything from a blob or button of moss, like this fragment about Thumbs, to an extensive stretch, as in those essays of the third volume, where time and weathering have made the moss appear a mellow feature of the wall itself.

III

Now if we consider the subjects in our present collection, we find a diversity different from Montaigne's in the choice and treatment of them. It is not only that the styles and outlooks of the authors vary, but their ages vary (with a lower limit of twenty-two)—and age is important in an essayist. There are certain qualities and indulgences—or, we may put it, certain defects and virtues—that are attainable and suitable in middle age. "That young man should deserve the whip", says Montaigne, "who would spend his time in choosing out the neatest wine and best sauces." On the other hand, let us say that elderly man should deserve scorpions who would spend his time railing at the bygone enemies of his greener days. Since I believe there are no elderly men in this volume, we shall have to select Edmund Blunden (who, although not middle-aged, terms himself a young ancient) as an example of the reconciled spirit. For, having had no thumbs cut off by a cautious parent to prevent his going to war, he now recalls his companions in that ordeal with so happy an affection and in so rich and balanced a retrospect that we understand how sanity cancelled madness, and how existence, even in the trenches, was a chequered business lit up by fine understanding.

But are we to prohibit all controversial themes to an essayist because they imply some form of enmity? Montaigne is too hard about this question when he declares, "There is no passion so much transports the sinceritie of judgment as doth anger". We have only to read Naomi Mitchison's essay to agree that her sincerity of judgment is not transported. The reason is that her anger against books is conditioned by facts and qualified by wisdom. It is a carefully weighed anger, and most of us have felt it, without being able to inquire into the matter with such control and clarity. Besides, Bacon is on our side as erring humans when he says, "To seek to extinguish anger utterly is but a bravery of the Stoics". Accepting this, Peter Fleming allows himself a fling of quiet anger against certain conventional stupidities; but his skill and grace of personal confession are such that he appears to focus the criticism on himself. It is for us who read to make the readjustment, swinging the censure over to ourselves who were agog for the story of his search for Fawcett, without being too sure, perhaps, which river it was. Something of Montaigne is in this shrewd self-derogation; Montaigne would pursue it around

the classical isles where our modern traveller crosses the
Equator.

We may notice a lack amongst our essays of those idle and
vain subjects that can be played on like concertinas—stretched
out or compressed, made to emit high or low notes, unsus-
pected harmonies and erratic rhythms. Is it to be concluded
that our period is too earnest for frivolities? I think there is an
easier and less generalised explanation; one with more sense
in it, and more relevance to my own particular pleading. To
begin with, an idle and vain subject does not imply frivolities
by any rule or sequence: an essay on a mouth-organ may be
teeming with references to classical literature, just as a lament
for an old dressing-gown, like Diderot's, may be profound and
dignified. As I see this question of selecting subjects, it appears
to be mainly a question of whether you can, in fact, be wearing your old dressing-gown when the choice is made, or are
putting on respectable visiting clothes. Now a dressing-gown
is suitable wear in one's own study. By this I mean that anyone, sitting down to write a personal characteristic book of
essays in which only his own work—and plenty of it—will appear, is almost bound to have the ease and confidence that
will let him pitch on any manner of subject he comes across.
Like Montaigne's, some of the topics will be great ones and
redeem, as far as title is concerned, their modest brothers. But
it is exactly my complaint that books of essays have not been
encouraged. So I send out invitations, and although I attempt to add, "Come in your old dressing-gowns and sheep-
skin slippers, bring your favourite briar and don't trouble to
shave or have your hair waved (as the case may be)", I should
be doing the guests an injustice if I were to insist upon it. A
single appearance in a gathering cannot be so casual; the old
dressing-gown, that is merely a symbol of absorption and
comfort to the wearer in his study, is suspected by him to
denote slovenliness when outside his home.

This, I think, accounts for the rarity amongst this collection
of the digressive essay. Not one of the following pieces sets out

with a title that you gape at, wondering at its seeming triviality and barrenness, such as "Smells and Odours"; "On Nothing"; or, above all, "Thumbs". Yet we may pick out Kate O'Brien, who, beginning with the countryside as a subject, finds herself perpetually digressing because "the English landscape deprecates a too complete attention". What it has given her is a long smooth rhythm in which personal musing, snowdrops and reflective truths on country novelists are interwoven with peculiar happiness.

Its converse is the critical essay. Graham Greene, in treating of the religious sense of Henry James, and Richard Goodman, discussing the problem of D. H. Lawrence, set themselves a sterner and more rigorous task than the others. One may write on authors biographically and descriptively and be capricious enough; but each of these two pieces is, in the strict sense, "an essay of truth"—that is, of genuine criticism and interpretation, in which a writer cannot afford oddities and curiosities, but must keep (and does) a taut hold of his argument. As long as we have literature the critical essay will be indispensable. And there is no fear of the "all-is-said" attitude arising. Even if, to the disgrace of our posterity, it should arise concerning Shakespeare, T. S. Eliot or the Brontë sisters, there will always be new writers to be dissected. The eight volumes of the *Causeries du Lundi* need induce no sigh of repletion when it is realised that Ste. Beuve, for all his insight, could not write on Proust.

But what hackneyed and long-wearied subjects will an animated pen not pounce on and renew? If we are not content with Bacon as the final arbiter on love (and even his keenest words, *It is impossible to love and to be wise*, are borrowed), there is no lack of printed meditation on it since his era. But Michael Roberts has written a new essay on love; the mazes and mountains of his surprising discourse are no easy lurking-ground for hackneyed meditation, nor even for crystallized maxim or succinct design. In this satire on philosophic argument Michael Roberts—or let us rather say the learned

Gubbins—appears as an inverted Joubert, who can tabulate each word into a paragraph with huge enjoyment; and so long as we skip blithely through the paragraphs in Montaigne's manner, not plodding upon them to lose their own wit and effect, we shall find good sport from a gyrating intellect. Or we may have traditional subjects treated as tradition would warrant. Is it any the less pleasant to read "Sable Goddess" because we can picture Leigh Hunt writing something not unlike it for his *Indicator* a full century before Derek Hudson actually performed the job? There is no better argument against labels than these last two essays, the one seeming to prove that our young writers are all immoderate innovation, the other showing them as shamelessly tradition-bound.

Let an essayist be at ease in his own mind and neither tradition, protest nor originality need worry him. Certainly inhibitions should not. It may be a case of choosing the right background; and though Tangye Lean bewails that there is no right background, all surroundings being equally prohibitive to the writer, yet he writes. He goes on writing, with great gusto; even if, having rejected country, town and suburb, he keeps the location of his turret-room a secret. It is not so with Kate O'Brien, Philip Tomlinson and Adrian Bell, who, like true Britons, "venerate the plough", delighting to move, whether in fact or spirit, through the happy freedom of

> Leys and fallows, reedy rustling shallows,
> Colours and musics rustical.

For although our English essayists have had to choose town subjects—often for criticism and satire—when the din of Fleet Street was in their ears, still the country and the village have drawn them; even Addison of the coffee-house persuasion gaining his widest fame with a Gentleman of Worcestershire. Now we have the portrait of another squire from Adrian Bell, and it is to be noted that he is the *last* squire. Stubborn and tyrannical by long ancestry, a new influence works through him. He makes innovations, alters the aspect of the village, applies text-book theories of health and sanitation—and ends his race. The writer—whether poet or essayist—can no longer escape to a dreaming timelessness by leaving town. He still sees—perhaps by turning his back on a filling-station or a pink-tiled bungalow—the waving cornfields, the horse plough, or the comatose cow cropping grass in an upland meadow. But these pastorals are not static. A spectre pursues their indolence and simplicity. Urbanisation, mechanism and "progress" are driving them, as the conquering Romans drove the ancient British, into the remoter corners of their territory. As Philip Tomlinson comments in his Devon harmony of poets and landscape, "Some kind of fever in the blood, speed and jazz among its symptoms, presages destruction". And he notes the brave attempt to stay the enemy's onslaughts by cataloguing those features worth defending. It would appear that peace and contemplation are marked out almost suddenly for a violent death; defeated, as one country squire of Anglia has it, by the internal combustion engine, but let us say more generically by the hankering for speed at the expense of serenity. And what is at the back of speed (discounting its use by jaded organisms as a new sensation)? It is nothing but a poor attempt to defeat time, the enemy that is grinning at us in a hundred contortions. While we try to expand his hours, curve his course, and beat him at the winning post, each new intricacy of our invention chains us to him with a closer link.

We are caught up in a breathless dance of minutes; wheels revolve faster, news arrives sooner, sounds travel to more ears at the same instant, pictures dart in briefer flashes past our eyes. It seems to be no world for contemplative essayists, whose only remaining function, one might say, is to denounce and die.

But we do not die so easily, for we have been trained up in this school before. It is significant that James Laver, dealing thoughtfully—and, let us mark, unhurriedly, for his essay is the longest in the book—with this dilemma of the twentieth century, finds the root of our modern tyranny in Petrarch.

This triumph of the time-principle has been felt and known in the ages that we believed were leisured. Was life in any period comfortably static to those who lived it? Was there ever, outside a monastery garden, a place where the responsible adult could take his quiet motion from the diurnal sun and feel his duty sufficiently discharged? A century, two centuries ago, we find men complaining of the effort to keep up with modern life. The pace has always been a little breathless for man as a natural animal, and if it quickens now, his faculties quicken with it. He is not being outstripped, but he is strained into continuous effort, and there is no rest and solution except the harmony attained in his own mind. Not all of us can attain it, and not all the time; yet the poet has a solution to life's agonies, although by our stop-watch he has not defeated time and to our bodily perceptions he has not killed suffering. The essayist, too, without achieving that clear ringing note, makes an adjustment. He smooths out some wrinkles while we read him. He allays our restlessness by putting something right— not logically or argumentatively, for he is more often criticising than condoning, but by giving us a balanced and reflective moment. In it we may wander with his own thought, share his whims, and be caught up into his pattern. His very anger, which he may not "extinguish utterly", has in it a quality of justice and is free from haste. So we reach serenity through his outlook. Until there is no place for serenity and sanity on our planet, the essayist must be allowed his corner. He must have it the more decidedly to-day, when so few of us have leisure to indulge our green thoughts in a green shade unless—to put the matter crudely—we are paid for them.

Let us give the essay a chance to flourish, then. I am not suggesting that this present attempt will at once produce a race of essayists, even if it justifies my hope of making it an annual feature. But, to end these comments with a fable: An ambitious squirrel once began the task of emptying a pond by dipping its tail into the water and shaking out a few drops on the bank. Smith, pulling up on his way home from the "Jug and Bottle" to watch the queer experiment, pointed out the squirrel to Brown and remarked, "Mad". "Maybe he knows what he's about", Brown muttered doubtfully. But Robinson, coming up behind them, said, "Now if there was a thousand of them squirrels they'd empty it. Or, better still, ten men— and give 'em pails instead of tails to do it with".

THE COUNTRY

THE LAST SQUIRE   ADRIAN BELL

RETURN IN WINTER   KATE O'BRIEN

THE EARTH BEING TROUBLED   PHILIP TOMLINSON

THE LAST SQUIRE

THE curious prowler in this country churchyard would find it difficult to avoid him. His monument proclaims him, and there is no need to approach even within reading distance to know his station and period. The squire of course, and probably the last squire—the strawberry-coloured pillar of polished marble with its perfunctory little cross on top is so unmistakably Victorian, lording it garishly over the awry lichened headstones that positively seem to bow themselves. Aloof, railed about (against the living or the dead?), all but nature-defying, that polished marble. The other stones nature wins over to her harmony in time. By them not only are men's ages known but their endurance in memory is calculable. Children, grandchildren, even great-grandchildren may be assiduous in checking nature's approach, but in the end the delicate pattern of young ivy on the grey stone face is not disturbed, and it is left to the curious stranger to peel off the moss and read "Gone, but not forgotten".

On the north side of the squire's monument the weather has even managed to set its mark—a very faint greenness, which is a miracle considering the glassy surface, and a portent. But as yet it merely soils the marble. The squire maybe, and rightly, did not trust posterity to look after his memory, for he died an old man lamenting the times. All the same, his monument may be the least enduring of his memorials, for he left his mark on the village to an extent that no one person is ever likely to do again. Gone are the days when one man could alter local geography to suit his whim. Municipal administration and taxation ensure that. The village is Squire Park's true obituary. The history of the view from the churchyard much more than anything in it is a memorial to a vanished autocracy.

Why does the high road make that redundant detour?

Why that sudden depression in an otherwise smooth-sloping meadow? Why that row of brick cottages blinding the rectory windows?

There are various reasons given for the rolling of the English road, from primitive river-beds and jungle tracks to Mr Chesterton's picturesque assertion that the Englishman was drunk and that was his most direct way home. The cause of this particular double bend is just as human and a great deal more authentic.

Now that Squire Park has lain many years under his strawberry-coloured marble memorial, now that the village is governed even more peremptorily from Whitehall ministries, it is unanimously agreed with a sigh that Squire Park, "he was a rare good man". And it is added, more often than not, with a survey of the houses and the trees, "Look at all he did for the village, and little enough thanks he got for it all, as I've heard say".

Indeed, during his lifetime, his downright nature often distorted his aims to the popular view. A strong personality is often a storm centre, and with Squire Park it was certainly not only the good that was interred with his bones.

Wages were very low at that time—seven and sixpence a week for a labourer to feed wife and family on. Poaching was the inevitable result, and hatred of the squire's keepers by the lawless naturally extended to the squire himself. The Hall where he lived was a Georgian mansion abutting on to the road. That it did so was little enough inconvenience in those days of horse traffic, or would have been but that the aggrieved persons, when the squire and his lady were entertaining in their drawing-room, used to spit upon the windows as they passed.

It became insufferable; and the squire put a stop to it in the only way possible. He had the whole course of the road altered at his expense, so that it now curves sharply about two hundred yards from the Hall, curves again to pass it at a distance, and then two hundred yards beyond does another sharp double bend to resume its original course. The old road is now a private drive, and ample lawns intervene between the house and the highway. It is difficult to imagine, in these days of road improvement, a private individual being permitted to make four right-angle bends in a previously straight road to suit his convenience! Modern conditions have turned that half-mile into a chapter of social history.

But even privacy, under certain circumstances, can become relative. True, the working people could no longer insult the squire in his own house as they walked by, but a little way off, on the opposite slope, stood the rectory, facing the Hall. Not squarely facing it so much as obliquely squinting from an angle as though for the purpose of obtaining a view of what was going on in the squire's pleasure garden.

To anyone living in more populous parts it seems an exaggerated cause of complaint that another house can be seen from your windows, standing two fields away. But standards of amenity are comparative and local. The Englishman's home is still his castle; the last thing he will part with is his privacy. In a London flat he feels he has achieved isolation by being at the top of the building and immune from the annoyance of strangers' footsteps upon his ceiling. In the suburbs he who has been able to buy the next building plot and turn it into a garden has a sense of enhanced individuality; while trees, shrubs, walls and fences barricade every householder's few rods of ground, into which he digs his soul, from his neighbour's. So, in this sparsely populated region everyone is still agreed, if remonstrated with that it could hardly have been called a trespass on the squire's privacy that the rectory looked towards the Hall, that—"Why, the parson and his friends could see everything that went on down there". The rectory stood very little below the church that dominated the whole parish from its hill-top. To be overlooked by the house of God was one thing—by the house of His minister quite another. This did not really become a thorn in the squire's flesh till the old rector died. The new rector was a

sportsman, and the first thing he did was to retain the shooting
rights of his glebe land for himself, which his predecessor had
been only too pleased to let to the squire. This meant that the
rector was in the fortunate position of possessing an island in
the midst of one of the richest sporting estates in the country.
The glebe land thrust itself like a wedge towards the Hall from
the rectory. The rector appeared to be well up in all the tricks
of sporting agriculture, and the squire was incensed to observe crops of roots and mustard set right against his boundary
fences. On October mornings he would see, as he rode
round, a pageant of pheasants—his pheasants—decorating the
rector's stubbles. To all his friends he openly accused the
rector of scattering raisins—or plums as they are locally called
—to draw his game.

The rector had a cheerful but independent manner. Even
if Squire Park's opinions had not come to his ears, the great
man's frozen politeness, and the conflict between divine worship and personal antipathy on the keepers' faces in church,
should have spoken plainly enough. But the rector's round
pink face persistently apprehended nothing, and on week-days
from September to February double reports continued to ring
out just down there by the brook, startling the stillness of the
Hall precincts, and drawing the squire from his reading or
writing to the window, furious but fascinated.

It often seems that the sense of ownership is keenest in
regard to that property which is least amenable to the act of
possession. The partridge and pheasant wandering at will
have been and are still the cause of hotter disputes between
neighbours than the fixing of boundaries. To watch—and at
the sound of a gun the squire couldn't help watching—the
rector waist-high in mustard, bagging game which his keepers
had carefully reared, was too much.

Squire Park came to dislike the presence of the rectory over-
looking his gardens so much that it grew to seem as near to
him as the old high road had been. At length he offered to
give the rector as many acres as there are days in the year, if

he would agree to let him pull down the rectory and build him another one on the other side of the hill. As the rector's glebe was only seventy-five acres, he readily agreed to give it and the rectory up for a new house and three hundred and sixty-five acres at the edge of the estate. Or rather, he bargained for three hundred and sixty-six, because, he reminded the squire, it was leap year. So the old rectory was pulled down, its garden rooted up—the whole site ploughed, harrowed and set with meadow grass. The rector was put over the hill with a view that did not interfere with the Hall's. Only the cellars under the house remained, where also the well lay. This in time became a pond. Where the stairs down to it used to be, there is now a sloping way for the cattle to approach and drink; but the rest of the pond is railed off, because, the people say, it is so deep and the sides under the water are so sheer, that if a beast slipped in there it would drown. There is a sudden unnatural depression in the meadow, and that is where the rectory stood. So Squire Park achieved his privacy.

Under the old dispensation, the sense of personal integrity often extended from the man to his surroundings, nor did it stop satisfied necessarily at the house and its vistas. There was a sense of fitness, subtle in its recognition of comparative values; there were proper grades of amenity all down the scale. Wealth, and this instinct for wholeness within an area unified by a name or title-deed, achieved more in fact than the satisfaction of personal whims. It was the doctrine of "l'état c'est moi" in little, and when applied constructively it did at least provide an ordered human pattern as against the confused advance of the creed of "equal rights". One man ought not to be in the hands of another? But one man always will be in another's power—if not by force, then by rhetoric and persuasion. The man of sound is so rarely the man of substance, the demagogue is so absolute in his hour, that tyranny grows more vehement for being unavowed. Material standards are, after all, not so black as they are painted, nor

so barren of spiritual opportunity. The error lies in mistaking
the frame for the picture, in synonymising circumstances with
life.

The history of the Utopia-dream in relation to the English
village has yet to be written. You cannot go far without
coming upon visible signs of it, even to-day. That "Back to
Nature" period of Cowper, Thomson, Wordsworth, with its
sudden flowering of country sentiment, which like a too-
gleaming dawn was soon to be obscured by the smoke of the
industrial age, gave it impetus. Popularly the country tradition was a sentiment rather than a passion, though individual
lives demonstrated it to be their confession of faith. The antithesis of the socialist ideal, it yet came very near to it at times
in its creation of conditions of harmonious interdependence.
The cottage at the squire's gate was part of him in the same
way that his feet were part of his body, though they wore
leather while he used fine linen for his nose. The scale of social
values was analogous. One is far from pretending that, generally, there was anything ideal about those days. Economic
conditions among the peasants could hardly have been worse.
The last flare-up of independence had subsided. The machine-
breakings, the rick-burnings, the short-lived demand for a
living wage of half a crown a day, were over, and the labourer
was subdued. But these conflagrations had not failed to kindle
here and there a light that lived on. Lord Suffield's scheme
for the resettlement of the labourer on the land had been
apathetically received by the government, but individually
social awareness was not dead. The eighteenth-century mind
continued in country places; aristocratic, Horatian, assured
of its standards. It had no doubt as to the best design of life.
To laugh at its trickling grottoes is to confuse the decoration
with the spirit that inspired it. That was as the water that
flowed through the artificial cavern. A desire to civilise, without violating, nature, to meet in harmony on some half-way
line—man forgoing his luxury, she some of her wildness:
that aspiration of the country ideal stands up in social history

like some classic arch, sweepingly conceived, broken off in mid-air. There it stands alone in wild nature, a sudden articulation drowned by the wind, a lordly Folly in the yeoman's field.

As industrialism advanced, and towns grew large and smoke-darkened, the country idealist was the more concerned to keep himself to himself. Squire Park, at any rate, would not associate himself with the utilitarian culture; and, denied a general optimism, fell back upon building his world within his boundary.

He found support and inspiration in the writings of Ruskin, although he himself belonged to a past tradition. Curiously enough, after his death he was accused by realists of being "before his time". Actually he tried to build and leave a model of an older ideal, such as was swiftly being obliterated in the general world, to which, after the smoky ambitions of the times had subsided, men might turn again for a pattern. However, he did not scruple to make use of what the age offered; he was no mere romantic. Had he been so he would have let his cottages stay "picturesque". The thatch of the district toned with its stubbles—at the long view hamlet was hardly distinguishable from rick-yard. The porches of briar and eglantine, and within, the stooping beams supporting the low ceilings, the open hearths and small casements, were the very picture of Thomson's "tufted cottage". To the contemporary sentimentalist that at least was well. But the squire knew better. The true countryman is a realist after all, and his eye is so influenced by experience that he actually sees not the aesthetic harmony but the insalubriousness of such places. After all, a man is not a beast that he must live in a den in which he can hardly stand upright, and crawl into his sleeping quarters through a hole, not a door—not even a labourer earning seven and sixpence a week.

Squire Park was quite aware of what living in a two-roomed cottage of mud and thatch meant to a labourer and his family, although he himself lived in a spacious Hall; and since all that was his reflected upon him, it was as though his own boot leaked, or his sleeve was frayed. He was the first to censure any presumptuous fineness of dress among his servants, but the labourer in his mud cottage was definitely below the standard of plain sufficiency that made him to the squire's view, besides a servant, a type of human dignity—a man in his own right.

Squire Park, having moved the rectory, next pulled the cottages down and built new ones of red brick with red-tiled roofs in their stead, perfectly square, convenient, and graced, if not decoratively at least practically, with little brick porches like sentry boxes, having a seat on either side. The walls were of a double thickness of brick, the windows wide; instead of the old open chimneys there were cooking ranges in the living rooms, and wooden floors instead of brick. Moreover, the ceilings of the upper rooms were as exaggeratedly lofty as those of the old cottages were low, so that each room was about as tall as it was long, and this accounted for the extra height of the new houses in relation to the ground area. This was done with a purpose, for the squire knew how many of a large family had to sleep in a single room, and so he built the rooms high to be airy. In those days, too, there was a superstition that the "humours" of the night air were bad for health, so that bedroom windows were invariably kept closed, although six or seven persons might be sleeping within.

These houses were welcomed by the villagers. The loss of tradition was nothing to them compared with the gain in amenity. Squire Park was a practical idealist. He enlarged the gardens, too, for though his ideal stopped short of three acres and a cow, in theory he aimed at every man being self-supporting as far as possible, and in practice if any man expressed a desire for more land, he was provided with it. There are one or two farmers in the parish to-day whose fathers were labourers in the time of Squire Park, and who rose to independence by this means. He also built a brew-house containing a great copper for communal harvest brewing.

About this time there appears to have broken out another feud with the rector. No one to-day is quite certain what was the cause of it, some say a matter of church procedure, others that it was to do with the squire's favourite retriever getting caught in a trap on the rector's land. There are several "authentic" legends of how the quarrel arose, some showing that the squire, others that the rector, was to blame. There is no doubt that it was a grand flare-up, with the squire as passionately aroused as one brought up to rule by divine right of lineage can be when his authority is impugned.

He was considering a site for a new row of cottages, and in his wrath gave the order for them to be built right in front of the rectory, thereby cutting off the view of the country from the lower windows, and substituting one of back-doors and cabbage plots. No sooner were they completed than he repented, and the quarrel being resolved, and he and the rector being on the best of terms again, he offered, they say, to have the cottages pulled down and removed elsewhere. But the rector, not to be outdone in magnanimity, now that the tenants were all settled in comfortably and rejoicing in their new quarters, would not hear of them being disturbed. Squire Park therefore did what he could to make amends by planting a beech grove between the rectory and the row of cottages. There is one in the village who can just remember seeing Squire Park and the rector planting these trees together as an unofficial ceremony of reconciliation. Accord remained unbroken for many years after that. There was one further difference, but that was when both men were growing elderly and irritable. Again the precise cause is in doubt, but not the making of it up, for this was hampered by accidents.

The squire made the first advance, inviting the rector to one of his shooting parties as a tacit suggestion that bygones should be bygones. The rector accepted in the same spirit, and all would have been well but that Squire Park, being short-sighted, at the first drive shot the rector in the left buttock. The rector departed, swearing that it had been done on

purpose, and relations remained strained for a time. At length
the rector, recovering from his smart, invited the squire to
dinner. All went well till the squire, walking backwards in
saying good-night, fell into a new ornamental pond which the
rector had just had dug in front of the house. He dragged
himself out, accused the rector of a premeditated trick, and
stumped away home.

At length they met again and were finally reconciled at the
house of an intermediary.

But these petty feuds were incidental, and are only recalled
to show that personal differences often had a share in the de-
termination of village geography.

The new village shone out from among its trees where the
old village had crouched dun-coloured and indistinguishable
as a rabbit among meadow tufts. It found no answering note
of colour save in the roses in its gardens, and that occasional
wine-coloured sunset which is the shepherd's delight. But it
was alert, neat and new, and gave the people something to
live up to.

The "olde" and picturesque is the townsman's, never the
countryman's choice. The peasant in his antique porch is
merely a decorative symbol. He looks part of it but actually
has long outgrown it. By that curious tendency of civilisation
to return on its own tracks, only a sophisticated eye can now
visualise any ideal in thatch and plaster. It is a home of the
mind rather than of the body, a sanctuary, an escape from
the press of time. Enthusiasm for it implies a comprehensive
experience of modern life, and therefore, probably, a consciousness so stimulated that unless it definitely devotes itself
to the minutiae of nature, it will, after a period of rest, forsake
it again for the new environment. Hence, in many cases, the
week-end cottage.

The local poet, who was once the village harness-maker,
and is commemorated by a tablet in the church, having gained
a certain patronage and betaken himself to a more polite
neighbourhood, wrote wistful and affectionate verses in ab-

sence on his native place as it used to be. The thatched eaves,
the old hearth, the well, the woodland pool—the whole art-
less inventory is trotted gracefully out, until the reader too is
sighing for the "days that are no more". If only our poet had
returned and seen the change, and made a poem on that.
Those square, convenient houses: to this day their psychological effect is maintained. Though the integrating influence
is gone, the village is still reputedly an enlightened community.
Large windows made bright rooms, made the people bright.
With the old cottages it was a case of making the best of a bad
job. The wives definitely identified themselves with the new
ones. "They lovely housen" was, and is still, the opinion of
visitors from other more picturesque villages. "Wonderful
homely old places" they call their own villages; homely being
derogatory—higgledy-piggledy. And their antique homes they
describe as "downfally housen". It oppresses them to live in
them; they feel themselves a degree nearer the animals than
those who live in the new red houses.

Most villages have a central pump from which all drinking-
water is drawn, but this village went to a pool in a hazel
grove, called the Springs. It was small and only about a
bucket deep, yet in the dryest summer, no matter how many
dipped in it, the clear blue water always remained at the same
level. In a chalky, riverless country it was a miracle, that
small twinkling eye of water in the hazel thicket. The village
wells produced only "slopping water"—that is, fit for washing. How pure water is honoured in a waterless land as the
second great condition of life may be gauged by the tone in
which the Springs are spoken of. Wonderful properties are
adduced to the water that is fetched from there, almost one is
led to believe that men could live by it alone. It is never out
of the people's minds what a providential thing it is, that pool
in the hazel grove. The primroses blossom first at its edge;
the birds sing and nest earliest in the branches there. Were
Christianity not ingrained in them; did the church bells not
remind them once a week where God was to be sought, the

people would surely worship that pool in the thicket. In their hearts they probably do.

Squire Park had the water from the Springs laid on to the cottages he had built. He placed a great tank on a little hill above the grove. Two-handed pumps forced the water up from the pool into this, and pipes were laid connecting the tank with the cottages. The squire might have set up a wind-mill to pump the water, but as he had delayed as long as possible in introducing threshing-machines on to his farms, giving winter employment to men having them thresh with flails in the barns, so he thought it best the pumping should be done by hand, reserving it as a job for any out of work to keep the tank filled. If there were none unemployed, then the villagers had to agree to do it among themselves. They worked in relays at the pumps morning and evening, two and two. So the husbands pumped while the wives turned on taps, and none met at the pool among the hazels any more as they used, in the summer evenings especially, chatting and smoking as they waited to dip their pails. The path winding among the bushes became overgrown; the villagers came to take the water for granted, as though the pipes themselves were the source of it; and they ceased to talk of it.

There was one awful day not yet out of mind among the aged; a summer evening when all were working in their gardens or chatting at their gates. The squire's open carriage was seen approaching up the hill which was the village street, and on the box in frock coat and top-hat (he had been to a garden-party) the old squire himself, while his coachman (who had met a long-lost friend) lolled like a lord dead-drunk within. Stern and silent the squire drove up the street be-tween the aghast villagers. A week later the coachman de-parted, but just as the van-load of furniture was leaving, his small daughter ran from the house crying that they had for-gotten "the little yellow tap", thinking that without that there could be no water where they were going.

In later years, after Squire Park's death, something went

wrong with the pipes. There was no one to take the initiative any longer, and they were not repaired. On the hill stands the rusty tank and the pumps are idle. The people take their pails to the pool as they used to do, and meet and chat there on the mild evenings, and seeing the early primroses and the hazel catkins hanging like sunlit rain, and the quivering blue-clear water in its little hollow, tell each other again what wonderful good water that is, and what a blessing it is to the village to have a spring like that just a few minutes' walk from their doors.

When he had completed the new cottages and laid water to them from the Springs, Squire Park built a school as a memorial to his sister who had recently died. Universal education was as yet an ideal, rosy as it was distant. Squire Park was more concerned to teach local patriotism than a smattering of wider culture. Nor did it occur to him, any more than to other pioneers, to doubt that, having been taught to read, the people would raise themselves to the level of standard literature rather than that standard literature would lower itself to theirs. Anyhow he was a realist to this extent; since the lives of the majority would be spent in their parish he considered it less important that they should know the capitals of the world than what lay at their own doors. The history and geography they learnt was mostly local, but it gave them an added interest in their own environment.

Twopence a week was the nominal fee; and all attended. For in this one instance class barriers were set aside, and there was no social stigma in the rector's children taking lessons with the labourer's. At the same time the squire built a reading room, where in the evenings the older men would come to be taught to read and write. Some of them were satisfied if they could learn just to write their names. There is one who can still remember guiding the hands of aged men over the paper.

The squire himself was growing old, and was reminded of the fact by the death of his bailiff after several years' retirement, the one with whom he had planned and carried out all his schemes, a man whose life was distinguished by nothing but its complete immersion in and identification with his master's idyllic realism. It is said that after the funeral service the squire stayed in his pew sitting silently a long time, while the rector and the churchwarden and a few others waited in the porch. No one spoke to him or disturbed him, but they waited till he was ready to go.

He wintered abroad latterly, but his mind was still on his estate. He sent over trees, with explicit orders where they were to be planted—a wind-break of firs here, a coppice in an odd corner. He had a passion for trees, and spent his declining years in planting them. He would have made of every meadow a pleasance, for he conceived that no pasture was complete without its shade.

He planted oaks and elms, walnut trees, and along by the brook, willows. The men who helped to plant the latter, or who played as boys among them, still speak in topographical reference of "the willows", though they have since been sold and felled, and to the stranger are not in existence.

Squire Park's last act was to plant an avenue of limes along the road from the Hall to the church, "so that", he said, "my son will be able to walk along an avenue of trees to church on Sundays". The avenue is just coming into maturity, but Squire Park so impoverished himself by his improvements that when he died his son had to sell the estate to pay the death-duties.

The Hall is now a farm-house, the county council has taken over the school; and has done what it could with the four bends Squire Park made in the road. But even so they achieve a slowing up of traffic to-day, so that nothing passes that way through the village at more than twenty miles an hour. In summer the cattle lie under the shade of the oak trees in the meadows, and later the village youths stand poised with pliant poles whipping the walnuts from the walnut trees. In the brew-house communal brewing continues annually with that famous water, and the erect bright red houses are still the envy of labourers' wives.

Now that housing schemes, educational reforms, the re-suscitation of village life, are all under daily discussion, it is the general opinion that Squire Park was before his time. He was, it appears, a socialist, according to local capitalist opinion. Largely, one gathers, because everything he did was uneconomic. "Look at those houses", they say. Good? Too good. And the water and all. Even the maximum rent the labourer can afford couldn't pay a quarter of the interest on the money. Even viewed from the point of philanthropy there was nothing in it. "What thanks did the people ever give him for all that he did for them?"

Well, perpetual gratitude is not a quality of the robust. The worse if it were. Squire Park lived his idea; that was his good fortune. Possibly the people are neither more nor less moral, thrifty, God-fearing than they were before. Where, then, was the good? Materially, at least, it is still there.

RETURN IN WINTER

THE rural habit has always been, intermittently, an urban fad, but never in such wide extension as in this century, which has made week-enders of us all. Every man in his humour and seeking his especial need, we have learnt to travel, or to hanker, outwards now on Saturday. Outwards from the confines of town and suburb and from the barriers of ourselves. For though the absolute introvert will defensively seek and stay in the country merely because it is depopulated, his less hardened sympathiser, though of more or less similar inclination, will know that nature makes good contemplatives of those who have first looked outward to contemplate her. And all the rest of us, who have little time or hope to extend our souls, still wish now and then to observe the ways of quietude, under a quiet sky. So, modishly and with much noise of telephoning and starting up, we arrange and set out upon our week-ends.

Since these have averagely little in them of what we might be guessed to have come seeking, they are pathetic. For surely, however merely gregarious or fidgety or snobbish the immediate reason of any week-end party may be, its essential is that it takes place in the country, thereby implying in its participants some other need than each other's encouraging society. We forget of course that wherever we go we take ourselves and that everything we desire may only be assimilated through that muddy filter. We forget that excellent things are not to be attained simply by dashing off to where they are said to be.

It is a limited truth that nothing is anything except by contrast. Contrast is, admittedly, a dramatiser, and the week-ender dramatises country life for himself by living in town. But the dramatic is ordinarily only a flash-in-the-pan way of

perception, hit or miss, and though the snowdrop, trembling
under eyes that yesterday and to-morrow are street-bound in
unawareness of her, is up to a point "good theatre", she is a
platitude as well. Her real quality is to be discovered only
out of knowledge of the cold grass before she came, and of its
coldness, subtly changed, after she is gone. For their place in
time, within their own sphere, is the significant point about
objects, as about ideas, more significant than their effect when
held for a moment against unrelated contemporary things.

But I write uneasily this morning, on a querulous note, as
if I had a grudge against week-enders, which—let my friends
witness—I have not. Nor against anything at present, unless
my fire which, now that the bullying east wind has left us, is
lazy about roaring up to warm my room. But even that is not
a grievance, since mildness, with all respect to last week's
snow-striped landscape, was a little overdue. My snowdrops,
for instance, whose early exquisiteness was in my mind a
paragraph ago, are growing sallow and defeated—too soon
even for them, whom the gods love greedily; and the lambs
immediately to be born in the next field will surely fare better
if their first breeze comes to them gently from the west. And
irrelevantly here I note, and observe all over again through
my window as I write, with what an excellent grace do sheep,
of all animals, suffer pregnancy! Those wool-wrapped ladies
over the fence, waiting placidly for their time, give almost no
sign at all, in line or movement, of their expectant state. This,
with the ludicrous beauty of their babes, seems to be their
only triumph over other females of the farm—for femininely
speaking, it can hardly seem to them worth debating whether
to make mutton and blankets is a better thing than to make
beef and leather.

But I was saying, or was about to arrive at saying, that rural
life is elusive of week-enders; because its rhythm is slow and
its progressions are almost intolerably drawn-out. Come back
to it recently after more than two years of life in town, I have
often been daunted in these first weeks by that of it which,

sentimentalist, I had forgotten—its inexpressiveness. It was winter when I came, and winter is only now beginning, reluctantly, to die. But it is our vogue—since we are in love with spareness, in love with elimination, a little in love with death, to make much of winter and to look attentively into its grave and moody face—so, when the thin light falls demurringly on the infinitely graded plain that spreads north-east from my windows in vague, small undulations until, rising with a little sweep to a last curve of trees and the broken, sad towers of a Norman fortress, it meets the sky, I am rewarded for patience in being able to see the England Gainsborough saw, and Cotman. For the low-toned immobility breaks under the least movement of light, and in the subtly hinted recessions, shadow and light and half-light and half-shadow, I can discover not only the muted beauty that is, but the uncertain prefiguring of what later may rouse itself to be. And then the light flits off, and the scene it touched folds up again.

That sort of thing is exasperating, but it keeps the faithful on the watch. "Had we but world enough and time", the week-ender might feel inclined to cry at it, but we who are in no hurry persist, as the poet did, in loving the withdrawn one. Indeed, with the English landscape we would not have it otherwise. For by its very unreadiness, which even spring will only succeed in coaxing to a lessened gaucherie, a kind of sweet discretion, it is itself and characterised. Its allure, which wells up slowly, must be watched, not glimpsed. And while we watch it keeps us guessing.

Keeps us guessing. That sounds vulgar—but discretion, true discretion, has no vulgarity in it. And what is the English landscape if not discreet? Discretion—that is what ennobles while it limits it; that is what makes it slow and chary of high moments, and keeps it unresponsive to the week-ender's hail and farewell. For brief visitation the tragic arrogance or tragic mysticism of the Irish scene has a much more certain gift, as has say the contemptuous nakedness of Spain or the suggestive, dramatic bleakness of the American prairie. But

in England, if you are not willing to sit as long as may be on a
gate, forgetting the little hills you stare at almost as completely as you forget the rabbit-hole down which your dog has
thrust himself; in England, if you are not able to think a little
of the past, if your memory does not shuffle easily backwards
towards dead poets, if you are not content with giving only
half your attention to what is spread before you—if in fact
you have come out to be astonished and to make great ex-
clamations, you have come to the wrong place.

This obviously contradicts the detraction, often levelled
against the English scene, that it is tame. It is only as tame
as its own smaller birds, who will bring their lovely antics
nearer and nearer to your garden chair, or to your open
window, only as by daily habit and by your obvious absent-
mindedness they grow to understand that, though less useful
to them, you are almost as mild a permanence as the elder-
bush they love to play and feed in. It is no use gushing at
blue-tits, but provided you never applaud you will sooner or
later be allowed a non-stop programme of acrobatics. But
not within the span of your week-end. Which reminds me that
it is most probably those tinkle-voiced tumblers who are tearing the young buds from my japonica. And yet, though one
must regret such havoc, I fear that I could never be as enthusiastic as a neighbour here, a real gardener, a walk round
whose garden at present is made laborious and a little slow by
having to lift pots and glass-bells from everything that is
worth seeing. The birds are her eternal enemies—and no one
on earth would blame her for guarding her exquisite Irish
Christmas rose against them—but when it comes to covering
up the primroses—well, for my part, I'd as soon have birds as
flowers in my garden, for I know nothing lovelier. Which is
easy to say since my garden, though old and promising, is a
stranger to me yet, and bare. The winter aconite has gone,
and so have the three dark rosebuds that stayed all through
the snow, closed up in hardened innocence, and fell at last,
still frozen virgins. The jasmine has shrivelled, and the ugly

shrub with the glorious name, Rose of Sharon, is a muddle of
dark green and dreary brown. The snowdrops, as I have said,
are no longer beautiful, and only winter heliotrope remains
to companion the sharp crocuses and the eternal primrose.
They, with the pinkish buds of laurestinus, the tattered silver
of honesty, the grey of lavender and camomile, the shooting
green promise of daffodil and iris, are almost all my garden
has to offer yet, with yellowish grass and dowdy catkins. But
the birds are everywhere—their red and black and white and
blue and buff and pink and grey—speckle and flutter and
twitter and chirrup—they are just now the high notes of the
garden, flowers that have the nerve to toss about and sing
when all the rest of life is only turning in its sleep—the very
morning stars of spring. I do not think that I will ever buy
a bell-jar. Which only shows that I will never be a gardener—
though I like the sound of gardener's lore, and was touched
the other day to find that John Evelyn, in his *Directions For
His Gardiner*, told that happily instructed man that "to have
stock Gillyflowers very faire, choose a plant which beares excellent double flowers, suffering it to beare but only one
branch of flowers; save and sow the seedes of those flowers in
February on the Hot-bed, and plant them forth in Michaelmas: This is a precious seacret". So precious has he made it
sound that, had one a hot-bed and were one equal to the
effort of paraphrasing for a twentieth-century labourer his
rarely styled instructions—since the lovely book may never
reach the tool-shed—one might attempt to have gillyflowers
"very faire". But one came here to work at another job than
gardening, and Evelyn must not be allowed to play side-
tracker. Besides it has always seemed to me that gillyflowers
are fair, if you let them be.

To-day however I seem to be my own side-tracker.
A friendly neighbour—she of the bell-jars—said to me the
other day: "What on earth brought you to live down here?"
She is Irish and has been for forty years an exile, as her heart
insists, in East Anglia. Although her garden is very beautiful

and mainly the work of her own soul and hands, and although
she inhabits a house that began its life in the fourteenth century, she refuses, in conversation anyhow, to see beauty hereabouts. "What in the name of God", she said—she is vain of
her brogue—"brought you to this outlandish spot?" "Well,"
I murmured, "it's beautiful, isn't it?" "What's beautiful,
will you tell me?" I was at a loss, because it is beautiful, but
it wears so much its dress of inexpressiveness. "Ploughed
fields", I suggested timidly. "Yah, what are they? Wouldn't
you like a big mountain better, or a great river, or the sights
you'd see on the Bog of Allen?"

I might, sometimes. I was born beside a great river and in
sight of mountains which, if not exactly Alps, yet wore snow
on their heads sometimes for six months of the year. I was
born within an easy pony-drive from boglands. I know those
wild and easily triumphant beauties, know them far better,
I suppose, than I shall ever know this soft East Anglia. For
the knowledge we are born to is probably the only kind that
can never leave us wholly. Miss Theodora Bosanquet, in her
recent exciting and too short book on Paul Valéry, says that
"it is their rare susceptibility to early impressions that makes
it hard for poets to grow away from their infancy. The form
and scent and colour of the world that was about them when
they were children persist so durably that they may seem to
play all the drama of their mental life against that back-
cloth". But poets are after all only men, men extended and
fully used, and their susceptibilities, of which they make their
tools, are also in some measure ours though we do not know
how to forge and burnish them. But it is true that what we
had when we were children we have for ever, and when we
choose to look attentively into our early years we see that for
good or ill there is no such thing as exile from them. However, this did not seem an easy thesis to develop by the tea-
table of a new acquaintance, although I would have liked to
suggest to my fellow-countrywoman that to have grown old
lamenting her mother's garden and the woods beyond it, to

have spent forty years desiring the Bog of Allen and the Wicklow mountains was a surer way of possession than to have lived beside them, though perhaps not so satisfactory as to have exorcised them through poetic creativeness. But her answer would almost certainly have been a contemptuous "Yah!"

How I digress, who set myself to talk of that which lies about me! But from that one will, I suppose, perpetually digress, for a thousand reasons, and among them one which I have already mentioned—that the English landscape deprecates a too complete attention. To-day however—a windier day than yesterday, so that the garden proved no place at all to read the morning paper in, and my study fire, behaving better, suggested no legitimate escape from work—to-day I thought I had some reasonably intelligent observations to set down here about the English scene in relation to the English writer, about the relation of temperateness to impulse; and, seeking support for some small point among my bookshelves, I came, accidentally, upon the letters of Cowper. That was nearly three hours ago, and now the best hours of the working day are gone, and I have spent them lazily at Olney, in the greenhouse, in the garden, in the parlour. And by this inexcusable digression I find my theories both supported and refuted. For, if discretion is a key quality of English landscape, taking the word with metathetical vagueness, and if we dare relate its restrained but truly noble suggestiveness to the niggling and flat mannerisms of the countryside of Olney, then undoubtedly it was something of that quality in his surroundings which kept an unhappy poet pseudo-happy when a more inflaming and exacting scene must have undone him; but on the other hand, if English landscape rejects a too close attention, what are we to make of the insistent tender watch which Cowper kept on the little movements and changes of rural life in relation to the felicity which was that watchfulness' reward? But perhaps he did not really stare so very hard in the plain man sense—hard enough to lose the whole in the parts, that is. A poet, he only needed the outer world to hint and whisper a little with his muse; it was in his letters and recreations that he allowed himself his gentle inquisitions. He knew how to look at things, and also how to ignore them. " . . . They desired to see the garden and greenhouse. I am proud of neither, except in poetry, because there I can fib without lying, and represent them better than they are."

To fib without lying—that is the creative writer's job. To succeed in it he must have at his disposal a field of special knowledge—never mind how untilled and forgotten, so long as it is there and is especial to him in the sense that only he, in his bones, and by the accidents of personality which make him himself, can have that special knowledge. Over that field, without ever coming to know its extent or its whole composition, judgment will exercise selectiveness, and the quality of the resultant work will depend on two things, the worth of the unknown factor, the uncharted field, and the tact, both submissive and imperious, of the functioning judgment. It is work done in the dark, really. It is as if something known only to one-half of a creating spirit is stirred into discomfort by some other thing seen outwardly by the whole man, the task being then to release it in a form as analogous as may be to the form of that which had disturbed it, so that from being itself and hidden it may by chance take on a universal life. It is the turning of a personal and quite unprovable truth into a generally recognisable image. It is, in fact, to fib without lying, since it is to pass off to the world as generally visible that which by its nature is unique. Which is all that any writer can do, and, thus stated, hardly seems worth doing.

To which a writer would probably answer that the trouble is that—by one of the accidents of personality which make him himself and which is hidden in that field of special knowledge which his judgment will never quite encompass—it must be done. Unaccountable disturbances recur which make the not-doing unbearable. Things seen are lighted by unseen and unremembered things; faces, gestures, patterns, emotions press on a nerve whose untraced terminals set up an ache which only the effort of discovery and manipulation into form can ease.

This granted, it is for the writer to find a dwelling-place, an atmosphere wherein, for some reason which may be quite simple or entirely esoteric, the stimulating nerve-jolts will not only take place with frequency but will be more or less safe from the bromide effect of irrelevant impressions; in other words, as they recur judgment must be disengaged, alert to exercise its selective and tactical function upon them. And although it is pretty safe to say, at least of writers of fiction, that the most memorable of them made themselves remembered because, for one good reason, they found a *pays* which analogised nearly and deeply to the hidden country of themselves, and which rewarded them with their own best work. This sympathetic country which vitalised their hidden nerves may or may not have been their native place, and when they used it as their vessel they may or may not have found it best to live with it—the only important thing so far being that they had found it. The next point would have been to discover, by self-examination, where they could best relate this *pays* to that in themselves which gave it its significance. There are writers who can only take command of their murmuring purpose when all the roar of life is round their heads and no impression static; others who, to re-create that very confusion, must fly from it. Some writers want their *pays* underneath their eyes; some close their eyes to find it. There is no rule. Hardy stayed in Wessex, but James Joyce lives in Paris. And in the vein of the gentleman who said that Mr Gladstone was dead, the Queen failing, and he didn't feel very well himself, one seems to have discovered that the impulse to work, always elusive, comes most frequently when life is cast in country routine, in a setting which, neither ugly nor shatteringly beautiful, is tranquil, subtle-mooded and worth intermittent observation. The characteristic English landscape, in fact, which, sunlit now and filling my open

window, is rich in promise that is not all illusion. For at least
one supposes that, short of dying, one will be here awhile,
working or idle, while the slow and lovely phases that it has
to undergo sweep over it—and that idea is both soothing and
provocative. Knowing oneself even a little, one knows that
nothing, or worse than nothing, may come out of this deliberately chosen peace, this mannered and discreet suggestiveness—but at least one will have seen the march of the English
year again. The orchard grass will be renewed and will stand
erect, each blade a lance, and then droop over, lazily, for
summer; the orchard blossoms will shoot into the sky, and fall
away like fireworks; after the daffodils the swifts will come
and the ewe-flock will go crying to be sheared; when the hay
is in and the nightingale is quiet, when the cuckoo's two notes
change to three, there will still be roses; bats will wheel then
in the dusky garden and moths will fight their tragic battle
round late-lighted candles; slowly, slowly we will approach
the burnished corner of the year.

These eternally repetitive things have no monotony, and
do not have to dodge that menace, as the novelties of the town
are forced to. It does not matter how often other eyes have
observed the sudden flight of wild geese above river meadows
or how many times one has eavesdropped oneself on the can-
tankerous conversation of moorhens; there can never be an
end to noting the tricks of evening light, or to counting the
number of sounds that go to make up silence. These games
retain their quality, and the walks on which they are played—
and best played in solitude—are the better for having been
made a dozen times. For then a deep familiarity gives every
change its true significance, as distinct from its immediate and
obvious effect, which is all that a week-ender gets.

Though undeniably a week-ender does get something.
Once on a wettish autumn Sunday I was taking some friends
through a leafless wood in Kent when we found a dead mole
in our path. One of them lingered behind us, staring dreamily
at the little corpse, and as I waited I heard her murmuring in

gentle astonishment: "A real bit of moleskin!" Which bears out my theory that for brief visitation the country is good theatre.

For certain novelists what we may call the rural, as opposed to the urban, fact has been the essentially decisive thing, the key to their discovery of their own purpose, that which set them free to themselves. For though one can easily enough imagine Thomas Hardy as a novelist, had he never seen Egdon Heath or the great plain that lies between Christminster and Shaston, it is impossible to imagine that T. F. Powys, for instance, could ever have fitted his great fables of good and evil to any other but the biblical formula of country life. A great many country novels are only country novels by accident—which is not to say that they are any the worse for that, though one could go on to argue that unless the foundation of a book persuades us of its especial inevitability, unless it is inalienably rooted in its *pays*, it is, in the measure of that non-inevitableness, unimportant. It is doubtful praise of any work of art to say that its appeal to all is easy. The greater a writer the more that is new and foreign to us will he bring, the more that is ineradicably his and is only somewhat revealed to us by the urgency of his impulsion. Shakespeare was never very much interested in presenting the natural man whom everyone could recognise with safety. His greatest creatures come from a region of conflict which most of us are content to leave unidentified. Lear, Hamlet, Prospero, Caliban—what is their kinship with our everydayness, our pedestrianism? It is enough that we have been forced to look at them and feel uneasy. With Dostoievski's people too we must feel this—as, in a rather different way, with Tolstoy's. Though then we can excuse ourselves that they are Russians. Which happens also to be a sound excuse, so far as it goes. But Jude and Tess are in our own dimensions, and we feel safer with them than we do with Falstaff. So it seems to me that in the measure in which Mr T. F. Powys gives us characters and crises from which our rule of thumb knowledge of our fellows jibs away, he is measuring his step in the footprints of the giants. And for the making of his vast attempt he seems to have found in the rural fact exactly the material his spirit needed. His sinners and devils and fools and gossips could never have had any other life but by their own hedgerows, in their own whispering cottages. Their setting is their inevitability; outside of it they could never play their grotesque fables through, and it is their author's triumph, as it is of Sean O'Casey too—another who hunts with the mighty—that he has found the *pays* which best gives back to him the angry, despairing music of his own spirit. What he takes from rural things is outwardly the antithesis of what Cowper took, though for both there is conflict with a devil, and each has sought to fib without lying. For though the man in the street will say that villagers are not as Mr Powys sees them, both poets know good and evil are too terrible to reveal themselves to the man in the street. But without them and without visionaries to behold them there would soon be an end to all creativeness, since they happen to be the stuff out of which the arts are made. Which makes one wonder whether, since moral conflict is being banished from the towns, since there there are no longer ten commandments and men have forgotten the discomfort of feeling guilty, whatever is left to be said about human entanglement may not have to be sought for in the country, where the categorical imperative still has vigour left to make assault on individual impulse. Here too, in these quiet places, may be the last hiding-place of comedy, for where nothing is wrong nothing is funny—and even of conversation, for where nothing matters, what is there to talk about?

The country, in fact, may be about to turn the tables on the town, for since manners always follow morals and the latter are now in hot flight from streets and squares, may it not be that soon we shall have to beat the rural solitudes in search of those graces hitherto called civilised? If that is so, there is small need to be querulous and captious with week-enders, whose prophetic souls are perhaps already setting nets for what they know they must not lose. Let them come then, on their brief escapes from the life of uniform. In their haunts individualism is dying, and they know it. Eccentrics have no longer a news value, save in the moment when they innovate what is to be a variation of the uniform. We march in battalions now—I almost said we march in gossips' columns. Discretion, once so urbane, has forsaken the vulgarities of Regent Street, and has returned to dream in her *pays*, the English landscape. Here still, in spite of many spreading sins against her, she has a space of safety; here still she has a chance to control and quiet us. No wonder we come back to the fields now, if we can; no wonder that if we can't we are week-enders.

THE EARTH BEING TROUBLED

A BOOK of pictures and a catalogue of names had caused the disquiet. It was some years since we had seen the purple and dun of the moors that stretch from Bampton to Porlock, from Winsford to Morthoe, or the sombre, less orthodox beauty of the other moors from Ivybridge to Oxehampton, from Bovey to Launceston; the villages whose cottage designs need take no shame from the architectural charms of the Cotswolds; the rivers and brooks whose very names have an exorcising sound when deleterious thoughts obsess. There was no hurry to revisit them while memory retained their assurance of tranquillity and well-being in a world of unrest. Their genial images were cloistral refuges, and meant safety. There was an inn farm on an unfrequented road which had been built by workmen in Tudor days who were poets in their way: the inn matched the deep seclusion of the farm, and was autumn-coloured by the friendly years. But the keen eye of one of our conquerors who was harrying the West had seen possibilities in this gem which never could have occurred to the rustic dullards who made it. He annexed the inn, converted the barns into dance rooms and the farm lands into golf links, and brightened up the landscape with chromatic notice boards. It is now "Half-Way House", where charabancs and motor-cars rest joyful travellers on their way from one dance hall to the next. Not far off we can consider the pylons how they grow. The sense of age and fulfilment is increased by the iron straddles and festoons of the Electricity Commissioners. We had heard all this, but nursed still a secret hope, for there was news that two miles of holiday huts which had made what was a glorious reach of coast take on the appearance of a large poultry run had been swallowed by the angry sea. Not a wrack was left by Nature in her gesture of retribution. In the slow workings of time dark oblivion would, it was opined, absorb the traces of our foolish activities.

Cold comfort, for here is this disturbing catalogue, bringing fearsome foreshadowings that barbarism may win the struggle, though it perish ultimately in the general ruin of its victory. Here, compiled by a real and anxious patriot, is a documentation of Devon's landscape and antiquities, giving, for those who need it, ready pictorial arguments for their faith in natural beauty, and, for the unthinking, a warning of precious possessions imperilled—an evaluation of local features which the Council for the Preservation of Rural England mark as in need of protection from the unheeding hand of change, wasteful "development" and exploitation. It is severely practical in taking stock of assets we still possess, so that everything shall be known for consideration when development plans are being prepared, and reminds us of hundreds of matters of importance in contribution to what is becoming a national debate. It appears to be argued by those who genuinely wish to save our inheritance that the conditions which determine beauty of landscape must be discovered and defined if guidance is to be given on measures of preservation. But what if the spirit should be dying which enjoyed and cultivated that beauty? And the plea may concede too much to what some may believe should be denounced without compromise as vandalism. What if it be true that scenic (or any other) beauty is the creation of the observer and does not exist as an absolute apart from his thoughts? This is a desideratum most devastating to pious and conservative minds; yet, if destruction is inevitable in the unstately march of mechanisation, it may not be without its consolation if we live long enough to witness the final extinction of the English scene. A field of corn, after all, is as utilitarian as a row of pylons. Is it only thinking that makes one a picture of loveliness and the other an outrageous incongruity? The poet of the future who stands tip-toe upon the last unbuilt-on little hill, will his heart leap up when he beholds the symmetry and colour of a field of petrol pumps? Then we may destroy what is left of our heritage of Arcady with a will.

But the poet of to-day, what has he to say? Can he look at the symbols of our time, as his predecessors looked at earth and sky, with vivid apprehension and identification and find in them interpretations of the unknown? The waste lands he sees, so far as we can discover, draw from him nothing but a whimper. Up to now, at least, he has not felt the signs of our times as the elder poets, old-fashioned sentimentalists that they were, felt the subjects of their inspiration in Nature, animate or inanimate, as though all matter were charged with consciousness, making contact with the living rock, hearing and understanding the resigned lispings of autumn leaves as they fell, or staring with a wild surmise at dawns that promised and storms that warned. Instead of artistic self-dominion in expressions of peace or protest we have now a wilful disdain of elegance to match the desert of cynicism. The few poets who have not betrayed us, who are impelled by affection for that nobler spirit of England that dwells in her fields and hills, her woods and streams and hedgerows, in her homes and the quiet works of her children, who have faith, if mistaken, in the indestructibility of anything that once adorned the world, are derided as but poor pastoralists.

A clarion call from the poets is needed on behalf of our English dower. The trumpet of a Shelleyan prophecy might, perhaps, bring down the walls of Jericho. If no one can sound it to-day, we must fall back on the old "unacknowledged legislators". The catalogue of the S.P.R.E. is excellent in its enumeration of assets still remaining, but a literary annotation would not be without its usefulness. And Devon can offer an enthralling one. It is not possible to shut out the scene without shutting out the poets. We recall that Izaak Walton, turning for a passing distraction from the streams he ennobled, in such elaborate simplicities of art and piety, to more studious but not less endearing sympathies, opens one of his most animated characterisations of men of learning and ingenuity with the words:

It is not to be doubted but that Richard Hooker was born at Heavy-tree, near, or within the precincts, or in the city of Exeter; a city which may justly boast that it was the birthplace of him, and Sir Thomas Bodley; as, indeed, the county may, in which it stands, that it hath furnished this nation with Bishop Jewell, Sir Francis Drake, Sir Walter Raleigh, and many others memorable for their valour and learning.

Thus he strikes the note to which our ears are now accustomed whenever the word Devon is uttered. But Drake and all the valorous men are forward in the histories and may be taken for granted. How many volumes of Hakluyt do the adventurers of this one county fill? Yet Devon has claims to a larger shelf in the English library. It would be a pleasant pursuit, but a long one, to investigate fully the literary inspirations of the county; it is not a question of names only, for it would be discovered that such inquiry went far into the larger harmonies and involved the affinity of the poet with the English feeling for Nature. Throughout our history there has been a quiet hand-in-hand comradeship between our people and the country scene. The individuality of mills and homes and barns and bridges and churches is one with the works of Nature, like the hedgerows. This genial understanding has been in the national culture since Saxon days, perhaps earlier.

Is it but a lucky accident that the traveller on the long road that lies between Torrington and Bideford, where high hedges afford scant outlook on surrounding rich varieties, comes suddenly upon a sharp turn where field gates on each side of the angle offer him two gleaming visions? He lingers long on these wonder gates: one looks across miles of field and woodland and moor to the summit of Dunkery; the other reveals the peak of Yes Tor and the dome of Belstone, with many satisfying glimpses of the Torridge and its luxuriant banks. Two old farm gates, and they perform a miracle. They were no accident; they were rather a consecration, the deed of a good landlord testifying like so many of his kind to the traditions of his forefathers.

Minds sensitive to our country's stature in history are aware that the best work of the poets forms a consonance with this co-operating genius. In this subtle unity is a glory which is not equalled elsewhere in the world; and the demand for preservation is more urgent than a mere sentiment: national and spiritual life may perish if the vision fade that made it illustrious. In moments of despondency at the swift march of a corrugated, alien progress it is to that vision we turn in hope that it will yet triumph. A superiority to a "pretty pastoralism" betrays bluntness both to the nature of poetry and to the nature of man. The glory in the grass is an ever-present theme and a continual refreshment in English verse. From the reaches of thought and the rich incantations of poetry and prose, all the subtle-knit elements of that true civilisation which dwells in the mind and in the heart, or dwells nowhere, how much is due to simple love of this green earth?

To speculate upon what the poets have sung of our real wealth may help to prepare the plans of a better state. As much as the beauty of their setting do the musical associations, with their spirit lore and earth lore, make magic of the names of Tavistock, Dean Prior, Ottery St Mary, Bideford and Barnstaple. To hear them is to hear the bells beyond; to be dull to their appeal may "ring the bells backward". Asphalt and corrugation may march in conquest till what once was Devon turns its pitiful, blind face to the sun. If this is progress, who shall "beat the drums for a retreat"? We may yet be driven to the practical sanity of the poets. In a literary annotation to this classification of endangered beauty spots it may seem to some a questionable reversal of the common view of practicalities to think immediately of Coleridge, chief of Devon's poets, whose impressionable childhood was spent at Ottery St Mary; but it is not too romantic a fancy to see the impulses of early days rustling through his mind in that small

and silent dell amid the hills of the adjoining county where
his poetry came to its short season of noble blossoming:

> The dell
> Bathed by the mist is fresh and delicate
> As vernal cornfield, or the unripe flax,
> When, through its half-transparent stalks, at eve,
> The level sunshine glimmers with green light.

It is to Ottery's honour that this masterly comprehensiveness
that makes one county all the world, in outward aspect and
inner spirit both, should have had its beginnings in her quiet
retreats. The enfolding sweep of his genius leads us to overlook that Coleridge, in his instinctive and exact apprehension
of natural scenery, his awareness of the "inward murmur"
and of the detail (as in that green light of sunshine through
half-transparent stalks) may be numbered in the front rank of
Nature poets. But there are lines when the inspiration is immediate from wistful memories of young dreams in Ottery,
"the spot where first I sprang to light". In the verses to his
brother George his yearning mind turns back to "the dwelling where his father dwelt", where were born "his wild
firstling lays". In those backward-looking visions the melancholy regrets for what the remorseless years had done to high
resolves were bathed in floods of amber light. The Otter
should, for Coleridge's sake and for another rich poet's, too,
be for all pilgrims a consecrated stream:

> Dear native brook! like Peace, so placidly
> Smoothing through fertile fields thy current meek!
> Dear native brook! where first young Poesy
> Stared wildly eager in her noon-tide dream....
> Dear native haunts!...
> Dear to Fancy's eye your varied scene
> Of wood, hill, dale, and sparkling brook between!
> Yet sweet to Fancy's ear the warbled song,
> That soars on Morning's wing your vales among.
> Scenes of my Hope!

The eyes of the young dreamer must often have been lifted
to the overhanging hill of Rockbeare, from whose crown can

be seen embracing views of the moors. We learn from the appendices to our catalogue of Devon treasures that twenty-one acres of that hill are, thanks to a generous donor, in the hands of the National Trust and known as "Prickly Pear Blossoms Park and Recreation Ground"—which suggests that a society for the preservation of ancient place-names may one day have to be organised.

We may stay awhile in the pleasant valley of the Otter, for names of the gifted family of Coleridge are abundant hereabouts. In Ottery did the father of S. T. C. try to save the souls of a stupefied congregation by quoting Hebrew at them —wherein we can see tracings of hereditary characteristics. But there is a more purposeful reason for lingering. In *Anima Poetae*, that neglected masterpiece, is a beguiling reference. An allusive and unfriendly remark on the Prince Henry elegy written by William Browne of Tavistock is followed by a note suggesting a charming concatenation: "Yet he is a dear fellow, that W. Browne who died at Ottery, and with whose family my own is united, or rather connected and acquainted". United, then connected, then acquainted is a delicious descent in exactitudes. It is not established to a certainty that the W. Browne who died at Ottery in 1645 was the Tavistock poet whose *Shepherd's Pipe* and *Britannia's Pastorals* are as verdant as the things they celebrate. (Swift, by the way, could be given an indisputable certificate of relationship; but to wander down all the corridors, to say nothing of making a catalogue of writers whose connection with the county is direct, might be to find Devon touching the literature of England at all points.) With Browne there can be no talk of subtle influences: the tribute to his native place is absolute and full-orbed. The local patriot need make no hesitant approach or nurse suspicious thought, as he may of Herrick. Browne, who knew the county north and south, for Barnstaple (which claims John Gay as son) comes into his story, made the songs of Tavy the songs of England. His British Arcadia is Devon entirely. His native town, sheltered in its woodlands, still sees beyond the

trees the bare moorland heights and hears the same music of
swift waters that enraptured Browne. To Tavy's "voiceful
stream" he confessed his debt for "more strains than from
my pipe can ever flow". His feeling for natural beauty was
Spenserian in quality, and his verse may be said to be
Spenserian in origin. He paid his dues to his mentor in a
noble passage. He was fanciful and, like Keats—a greater
master who disdained no instruction from a lesser—was pro-
fuse in ancient personifications and allegorical allusions,
sounding phrases and bold colourings ("I like the pleasing
cadence of a line Struck by the consort of the sacred Nine");
but at moments Clare himself, that rare interpreter, could get
no closer to the phenomena observed. The scented grove
yields bewitching aroma:

> Like to that smell which oft our sense descries
> Within a field which long unplowed lies,
> Somewhat before the setting of the sun;
> And where the rainbow in the horizon
> Doth pitch her tips; or as when in the prime,
> The earth being troubled with a drought long time,
> The head of heaven his spongy clouds doth strain,
> And throws into her lap a shower of rain;
> She sendeth up, conceived from the sun,
> A sweet perfume and exhalation.

The little Walla Brook that feeds the Tavy inspires a hundred
tuneful and affectionate pictures:

> Walla, the fairest nymph that haunts the woods,
> Walla, beloved of shepherds, fauns and floods,
> Walla, for whom the frolic satyrs pine,
> Walla, with whose fine foot the flowerets twine,
> Walla, of whom sweet birds their ditties move,
> Walla, the earth's delight and Tavy's love.

Pleasing cadences came to him in full measure from moorland
rills. He could make a breviary of endearing names alone:
"The Walla, Tamar, Exe and Tau; the Torridge, Otter,
Ockment, Dart and Plym". And not the least of the debts
that England owes to this poet is that he was a Preservation
Society in himself, as Herrick was. He was steeped in local

tradition, and there is a store of country scenes and customs
in his original mixture of fancy and actual fact. His heart
could expand, too, from that more obvious pride in the adventurers who "by their power made the Devon shore Mock
the proud Tagus". His county becomes all England in the
apostrophe:

> thou blessed plot
> Whose equal all the world affordeth not!
> Show me who can so many crystal rills,
> Such sweet-clothed valleys or aspiring hills,
> Such wood-ground, pastures, quarries, wealthy mines,
> Such rocks in whom the diamond fairly shines.

If the shape and movement of Browne's verses at times may
seem awkward to our sense, it should chasten us to recall how
high he stood in the regard of such nobility as his friends
Wither, who named him "the singer of the Western Main",
and Drayton, whose lovely lines in praise of the *Pastorals* could
be envied by any poet, however eminent. Nathaniel Car-
penter, in his eloquent *Geography*, praising famous men, en-
treated Browne, who had "already honoured his countrie in
his elegant and sweet Pastorals", further to grace it by drawing out the line of his poetic ancestors. We must regret that the
appeal was disregarded, or that the work is lost.

The ramifications of inquiry concerning these laureates of
Devon are endless. It may be merely sensitiveness to one of
the signal dates in history, and without importance, but there
does seem to the fancy terrific if unnameable significance in
the dedication by Browne of his second book of *Pastorals* to
William Herbert, Earl of Pembroke, in the year of Shakespeare's death. And the loving-cup continues its eternal round.
It passes to Milton. A copy of Browne's poems with annota-
tions by Milton is preserved; and the effect of the Tavistock
poet is clearly traceable in *Comus* and *Lycidas*. It is a cheering
and all but sure guess that Browne was in Herrick's company
at the "Triple Tun" under the chairmanship of Ben Jonson.
Herrick, fervid disciple of Jonson, was a Devon man perforce.
He submitted to adoption and looked askance at his home.

When his good-natured genius was wandering or asleep he
scolded it, as did Keats, with corrosive words. Did the local
gentry round Dean Prior, who enjoyed his "florid and witty
discourses", dream that their parson was petulant and home-
sick in their moors and vales while remembering lyric feasts
with Jonson? Once, tradition says, he betrayed his feelings—
rebuking a somnolent congregation by hurling his sermon at
them; and a gathering that could sleep through a pious address by Herrick surely deserved the choral scorn of all the
poets in England. Cromwell, who packed him off to the city
of his wistful yearnings, was blessed unawares:

> London my home is: though by hard fate sent
> Into a long and irksome banishment;
> For rather than I'le to the west return
> I'le beg of thee first here to have my urn.

Never was a dancing stream addressed with such incivility as
in the farewell to Deanbourn, that "rude river" by which he
had lived:

> Rockie thou art; and rockie we discover
> Thy men; and rockie are thy ways all over.
>
> .   .   .   .   .   .
>
> A people currish, churlish as the seas;
> And rude (almost) as rudest savages,
> With whom I did, and may re-sojourne, when
> Rockes turn to Rivers, Rivers turn to Men.

But the protest is too violent. Stones and men suffered no
metamorphosis when the Restoration sent Herrick back to
Dean Prior. Yet, perhaps, it was but a poet's fun. In spite of
more discontents in "this dull Devon-shire" than any since
his birth, truth compelled the testimony:

> Yet justly too I must confesse
> I ne'er invented such
> Ennobled numbers for the Presse
> Than where I loathed so much.

Only an ingrate would say less. The best of his versicles, those
that shine with most silvery perfection, telling of brooks, of
blossoms, birds and bowers, of flowers and may-poles, hock-

carts, wassails, wakes, of brides and bridegrooms, of youth and dews and rains, of Christmas and Twelfthtide, sports, ancient games and harvest homes, of all the "cleanly-wantonnesse" of country life, had their vernal source in Devon. Like Browne, he has embalmed for our pleased instruction many of the simpler greatnesses of England. He is not satisfactorily classifiable in the story of English song. We have to range from Catullus and Martial to Burns for comparisons—which means he was himself, just Herrick, an original, not to be labelled, except as the supreme lyrist of the Carolines. With Browne there was something of Wordsworth's approach to nature, on tip-toe as to a divinity; to the pagan Herrick she was a mistress, bright-eyed, charming, complaisant. He lived to his axiom, merrily and with his trust in good verses. And Devon was tolerant of his sly grimace, for when the eighteenth century had forgotten to place him among the poets, oral tradition at Dean Prior preserved his songs.

A transition to Keats is to the purpose, and not abrupt when Browne and Herrick are in the picture. The epistle section of Keats's 1817 volume proclaims a motto from *Britannia's Pastorals*; and reference has already been made to their fraternal delight in the rich word for its own dear sake. But Keats, with no years to spare, had farther to travel; life's problems would not let him rest content to sing only of Dryads in woods and Nymphs in the running streams, but the fruits of his keen young studies of the Tavistock poet are beyond guesswork. And he is closer to Devon than a poetic influence. The letter of gay fooling to James Rice about Dawlish Fair contains, as the late Miss Amy Lowell was able to establish, more stanzas than the well-known one beginning "Over the hill and over the dale". It goes on naughtily about the "debonnair" (odd adjective for such tricks) behaviour of Rantipole Betty, who "ran down a hill and kicked up her petticoats fairly". This drollery was Nature's benevolent relief at a time when Keats was passing through a valley of the shadow. Three days after the Dawlish song, the poet, saddened by that "flaw in happiness" which pierces beyond our bourn, indited the *Epistle to John Hamilton Reynolds*. Teignmouth can thus claim the birth of his ripeness. The visit was not otherwise propitious. During most of his stay the rain it rained every day. He struck the place with epithets: "splashy, rainy, misty, snowy, foggy, haily, floody, muddy, slipshod".

> The hills [he said] are very beautiful, when you get a sight of 'em—the primroses are out, but then you are in—the cliffs are of a fine deep colour, but then the clouds are continually vieing with them.

So he stayed under his roof to

> catch a sight flying between the showers; and, behold, I saw a pretty valley—pretty cliffs, pretty brooks, pretty meadows, pretty trees....The green is beautiful, as they say, and pity is that it is amphibious.

Keats gives no aid to the advertiser and the guide-books; but he confessed to three days of glad walks. Devon showed her fairest face; and there followed "some doggerell", as he named it, addressed to Haydon beginning "Here all the summer could I stay", and containing a catalogue of place-names: "there's a Bishop's teign and King's teign" and Coomb and the Brook and many another where

> The daisies blow
> And the primroses are waken'd,
> And violets white
> Sit in silver plight,
> And the green bud's as long as the spike end.

Unlike Herrick, he expressed at the last no gratitude to his hostess for favours; yet there were some happenings more notable than days of rain and doggerel: the preface to *Endymion* was written at Teignmouth, *The Pot of Basil* was finished there and, to crown all, what may be called the first fragment of his astounding maturity—*An Ode to Maia*.

It may be a labour not altogether unrewarded to search in the dramas of John Ford for the Devon birth-mark. Land lore works in a mysterious way. An analogy is not too far-fetched between the austere sublimity of his temper and the sombre majesty of Dartmoor, his early environment. We are on surer ground in turning to the ever-active Coleridges, who are never far, in person or in associations, from whatever scene is contemplated. Derwent, son of S. T. C., comes into contacts which ensue in curiously wandering tributaries. At Helston, in Cornwall, one eager-eyed boy who sat under him at the grammar school was singled out as his most distinguished pupil, whose loud affection for Devon in later years helped to create the need of Preservation Trusts. Charles Kingsley shares with Richard Blackmore, an adopted son of the West, the responsibility for piping to fascinated and innocent pilgrims, who flock to the shrines of their heroes, set up their bungaloid tabernacles and take there their everlasting unrest. Westward Ho! when Kingsley knew it was a place without a name. Until recently the church of Northam on its hill above saw but an imposing ridge of pebbles piled up by the Atlantic to divide one of the finest sand beaches in England from the flats and sand dunes of the Burrows; a cluster of small cottages; a range of cliffs, frowning and ominous in some lights, changing under restless skies to coloured clouds, almost diaphanous in seeming. The larger scene may or may not remain imperishable amid the activities of man; but it can lose its inner light and virtue under the jazz and tramplings of a giddy conquest. It is not to the disrepute of Kingsley if his romantic trumpetings end in a harvest of death; but it is a sad reflection that the memory of what was resplendent was not preserved in the writings of one possessing talents of exacter observation and that "something beyond sense". Blackmore comes much nearer to the secrets, but no more than Kingsley is he in the scale of those who thrill us with the larger harmonies. Between the steeps of Castle Rock and Foreland Point there did dwell, too short a while for our delight, one great spirit of full command and, in a life so short, of crowded programme and full performance. Lynmouth and Watersmeet have their part in the irradiation of Shelley's work; and, too, in the strange story of his earthly visitation. There he stayed for a while in his wanderings with Harriet, and there his servant was sent to prison for too admiring assiduity in the distribution of his master's prophetic seditions. We can rejoice that Watersmeet touched other Shelleyan chords which suffered no hardening from the animosities of politics.

It is another incident in Coleridgeana that carries us back across the two moors to the south again. In the house of George Coleridge, brother of S. T. C., there lived, while he attended school at Ottery, Richard Hurrell Froude, talented brother of that James Anthony whose historical inaccuracies may bother all tastes that cannot be moved by the pictures of the past his vivid mind evoked. J. A. Froude's art in colouring and symmetrical design was employed in generous measure in the story of Devon worthies; and he, who loved his county so, would have blessed the work of the National Trust in saving the noble headlands that guard his Salcombe. Froude and his heroes bring to mind another panegyrist, one John Prince, whose pleasant labours at Berry Pomeroy in the seventeenth century resulted in a gossipy *Worthies of Devon*, ancestor of a large progeny of county celebrations, at their head the graceful and learned *Biographia Borealis*, in which Hartley Coleridge, that fey genius of Devon stock, praises famous men of Yorkshire in essays that make modern escapades in psychological biography look pale and wan.

These literary considerations do not come into the book that has provoked them, but they are pertinent to its designs. Devon has not yet suffered as some counties have; but there are ominous signs of the despoiler. If inevitable change is not directed by the thoughtful plans outlined in this book, everything that makes Devon of joyous meaning will pass. It is not industrialism alone that now plays Caliban to the rural Ariel. Some kind of fever in the blood, speed and jazz among its symptoms, presages destruction. The earth has its rights and cannot be degraded and mutilated without a decline in the humanities. Careless of future fame, we are making strange emblems of our worth to outlast the living bones of Methuselah; centuries hence archaeologists digging in buried Exeters may uncover tin houses, petrol pumps and sparking plugs to exhibit as our marks, our symbols, all we shall be known by. There is the evidence yet, when the skies are friendly, that we journey on a jewelled planet of light. We may upset the balance of the gods. Can we travel round the sun on an asphalt ball?

BOOKS AND AUTHORS

FOOTNOTE TO LAWRENCE	RICHARD GOODMAN
HENRY JAMES—AN ASPECT	GRAHAM GREENE
ANGER AGAINST BOOKS	NAOMI MITCHISON

FOOTNOTE TO LAWRENCE

"And the man that is more than a man in you
Will wake at last from the clean forgetting
And stand up, and look about him,
Ready again for the business of being a man."
—Cipriano in *The Plumed Serpent*.

LAWRENCE was, in his own words, a "thought-adventurer". In his novels, poems, essays and sketches, he presented us with a report upon his adventuring, upon his explorations in human nature. These explorations were, of course, limited as all such explorations must be. In point of fact they were more limited than is usually the case and yet, contradictory as it may seem, it is just because of their unusual limitation that they are important. Most people by understanding much end by understanding nothing. Lawrence by understanding himself only, and this accidentally, led us to a more profound understanding of humanity in general. But, it will be objected, he said nothing psycho-analysts and other reformers have not said. In one way that is true. In his actual *statement* of existing disorders and conflicts he does say nothing more. But that is not the whole of Lawrence, it is only his negative side, his pointing out what was wrong. His positive side, his attempted solution of the problems with which he was faced, or, at least, his apprehension of a possible solution for these problems, went further. And this solution was one which did not point—as psycho-analysis seems to point, by attributing any characteristic which makes the individual really individual to the presence of a neurosis, complex or what not—to a humanity completely uniform when normal, but to a humanity of real individuals still preserving their own, and, at the same time, a normal, individuality. To attempt to outline this solution and the method of coming by it, and then to modify the former in the light of the latter, will be one of the aims of this essay.

4-2

The clue to Lawrence's solution lies, I believe, in Lawrence himself. Lawrence, it must be recognised from the first if we are to understand him, never got beyond himself. In his own phrase, he was "ego-bound". He never knew, never really understood anyone other than himself, and his understanding of himself was accidental. Those failings he saw, or rather thought he saw, and hated in others were really inverted projections of his own, and this was so because for himself he was perfect—a little god who could not be wrong. Of course, he did not realise this and always thought he was really understanding others, which is why I said his understanding of himself was accidental. What he did not understand about himself was that part of him which was not projected, the little Lawrence who was never at fault. Throughout his writing we can see this. In *Sons and Lovers*, Miriam is made to fail Paul Morel, whereas it is only too obvious that it is Paul himself who is really to blame. But Paul is the young Lawrence who, even then, is above reproach. *Kangaroo* tells us the same story. Somers and Kangaroo quarrel. Somers is right, Kangaroo is wrong. But there is more of the real Lawrence in Kangaroo than there is in Somers. Kangaroo wanted power, wanted to be a leader. So did Lawrence. The neat, quiet, often objectionably self-complacent little Richard who refused to be led is the unprojected Lawrence, the Lawrence we find in Lilly of *Aaron's Rod*, that side of his character which Lawrence admitted consciously to himself and allowed his friends to see. But behind this Lawrence lurked another and truer Lawrence, the Saviour Lawrence, the Lawrence who wanted to find a way of salvation from those whom he thought to be other people but who were, as we have seen, really the inverted projections of certain of his own characteristics. And in his turn this Saviour Lawrence was projected forth and another Saviour Lawrence arose who wanted to save from Lawrence the Saviour. So there was a regress and the regress was vicious and we are appalled by the tremendous futility of it all. Futile it was, because Lawrence was a man divided against himself and, being so, was powerless to accept his destiny and make it really his own. For the man who is whole is at one with his destiny and accepts it, because he is one with himself and accepts himself. The man divided against himself is, however, unable to accept his destiny and thus cannot truly be said to have a destiny at all. For him there is only a continual conflict between acceptance and rejection of that which might possibly have been his destiny, and futility is just this, the absence of a self-accepted destiny, with conflict for its correlate. Nevertheless, it is from this that the negative side of Lawrence's importance springs. He becomes for us an example, a far more vivid and touching example than is ever to be found in a psychologist's case book, of what should not be. It is not that he is different in kind from those individuals psychologists deal with and attempt to cure, but that by his writings he makes us realise, as no scientific report can, the tragedy and personal horror of it all. The moral of Lawrence in this negative aspect is that there must be no more Lawrence. The nearest conscious recognition of this is to be found in that great book, *Fantasia of the Unconscious*. But what at the present moment is important for us is to discover how and why it was that Lawrence was divided against himself.

Middleton Murry called his book on Lawrence *Son of Woman* and in so doing for once hit the Lawrence nail on the head. When we read *Sons and Lovers*, *Fantasia of the Unconscious*, and many of the poems, especially *The Virgin Mother* and *Spirits Summoned West*, we cannot help realising that Lawrence, like so many men, was a victim of what has come to be known as the Oedipus-Complex.

In *Fantasia* we find passages like the following:

If you want to see the real desirable wife-spirit, look at a mother with her boy of eighteen. How she serves him, how she stimulates him, how her true female self is his, is wife—submissive to him as never, never it could be to a husband. This is the quiescent flowering of a mature woman.

And this love of a mother for her son which "would have

been the richness and strength of her husband" is "poison to her boy". For the young man, tied to his mother by an ideal love-bond for life as a result of this misdirected wife-love, is rendered incapable of any sort of fulfilment in adult love. As Lawrence himself admits:

> The Parent-child love-mode excludes the possibility of the Man-and-woman love-mode.

And so it was in Lawrence's case. Listen to this passage from *Sons and Lovers*, following on the quarrel between Paul Morel and his mother over Miriam:

> "What is it, then—what is it, then, that matters to me?" she flashed.
>
> He knitted his brows with pain.
>
> "You are old, mother, and we're young."
>
> He only meant that the interests of *her* age were not the interests of his. But he realised the moment he had spoken that he had said the wrong thing.
>
> "Yes, I know it well—I am old. And therefore I may stand aside; I have nothing more to do with you. You only want me to wait on you—the rest is for Miriam."
>
> He could not bear it. Instinctively he realised that he was life to her. And, after all, she was the chief thing to him, the only supreme thing.
>
> "You know it isn't, mother, you know it isn't."
>
> She was moved to pity by his cry.
>
> "It looks a great deal like it", she said, half putting aside her despair.
>
> "No, mother—I really *don't* love her. I talk to her, but I want to come home to you."
>
> He had taken off his collar and tie, and rose, bare-throated, to go to bed. As he stooped to kiss his mother, she threw her arms round his neck, hid her face on his shoulder, and cried, in a whimpering voice, so unlike her own that he writhed in agony.
>
> "I can't bear it. I could let another woman—but not her. She'd leave me no room, not a bit of room——"
>
> And immediately he hated Miriam bitterly.
>
> "And I've never—you know, Paul—I've never had a husband —not really——"
>
> He stroked his mother's hair and his mouth was on her throat.
>
> "And she exults so in taking you from me—she's not like ordinary girls."

"Well, I don't love her, mother", he murmured, bowing his head and hiding his eyes on her shoulder in misery. His mother kissed him a long, fervent kiss.

"My boy!" she said, in a voice trembling with passionate love.

It is the old story: the mother who has never really been a wife, the virgin mother, as Lawrence calls her; her love for her son which compels him, by awaking the "great dynamic love flow", to love her and her alone, despite the verbal protestation that, of course, there must be another woman when the time comes—which it never does; the ideal love-bond which is never broken and which renders fulfilment in love for the son impossible.

"*On revient toujours à son premier amour.*" It sounds like a cynicism to-day. As if we really meant: "*On ne revient jamais à son premier amour*". But as a matter of fact, a man never leaves his first love, once the love is established.

The strange thing is, however, that although Lawrence recognised this as a general law he only half applied it to his own case. For he thought, as is shown in the *Look! We have come through!* poems, that he had broken the mother-spell in the struggle which engulfed him after his mother's death. But it was not as he thought. The truth is expressed in the poem called *The Virgin Mother*, where we read:

> My little love, my dearest,
> Twice you have issued me,
> Once from your womb, sweet mother,
> Once from your soul to be
> Free of all hearts, my darling,
> Of each heart's entrance free.
>
> And so, my love, my mother,
> I shall always be true to you.
> Twice I am born, my dearest:
> To life, and to death, in you;
> And this is the life hereafter
> Wherein I am true.

.   .   .   .

Is the last word now uttered?
Is the farewell said?
Spare me the strength to leave you
Now you are dead.
I go, but my soul lies helpless
Beside your bed.

All his life Lawrence was a divided man and, as a result, was incapable of finding fulfilment in love. The cause of his division was this mother-fixation. For by setting up an ideal love-bond between him and his mother, it brought about a disintegration of the proper unity of the man, leaving him only physically free, capable only of a physical coitus. And because of this he became aware that something was wrong in all his sexual relationships. It could not be himself, however, who was to blame for this. He himself was never at fault. Therefore it must be the woman. That was it! She was too mental. She asked for more in sex than should or, in fact, could be asked. It was the mind interfering in that in which it has no right to interfere. And so we come to the opposition which runs through and through Lawrence's thought, the opposition of the Body to the Mind.

However, before we actually consider this opposition, it must be noted that, in addition, Lawrence attributed a further fault to the woman: he accused her of trying to take upon herself the rôle of the male. Mellors in *Lady Chatterley's Lover* is made to voice this accusation in an extreme form when he asserts that women are "nearly all Lesbian". Lawrence condemns it as a perversion. It must be recognised he thinks that *maleness* and *femaleness* are two different modes and must therefore be kept distinct.

"Woman will never understand the depth of the spirit of purpose in man, his deeper spirit. And man will never understand the sacredness of feeling to woman."

What truth there is in this I am not sure. But there can be no doubt that Lawrence wanted passionately to realise, as he never did, his *own* maleness and it seems probable that here

again we have an instance of projection of his own failing.
Also because of his insistence on the body there would be a
temptation to base the distinction between maleness and
femaleness on the difference between the male and female
sex-organs, although I do not think that Lawrence can really
be accused of this latter naïve mistake. Nevertheless, it does
seem likely that, as some psychologists have pointed out, each
individual is by nature bi-sexual and then the actual sex of
the individual at any one moment would be that sex which
was dominant at that moment. But even if this were the case
we should not *try* to be of that sex opposite to what we are.

The opposition of the Body to the Mind, or better still, the
opposition, to use Lawrence's own mode of expression, of the
Sensual to the Ideal, was not I think primarily metaphysical,
although we seem to get that impression, especially from
Fantasia. I believe that fundamentally it was an ethical opposition and ethical in this way:

That which Lawrence for ever desired, but never attained,
was fulfilment in love; the real reason for his failure was
his disintegration, although he himself thought it to be the
woman's demand for that of which he was incapable, viz.,
complete, not merely physical, coitus. Then, since he considered himself to be without fault, this demand which he
could not meet must be a kind of perversion. Sexual inter-
course should be purely sensual, a matter of body. If you
make it more (and for Lawrence this meant letting the mind
interfere) you are sinning, not only against your partner, but
against your own sensual and essential nature. In sex, Body,
the sensual self, is good, Mind, the ideal self, is evil. Therefore
the sensual self is opposed to the ideal self, Body to Mind, as
dark is opposed to light, and Plato is reversed. So we read in
the last chapter of the *Fantasia*:

Sex is the polarisation of the individual blood in man towards
the individual blood in woman. And sex union means bringing into
connection the dynamic poles of sex in man and woman. In sex
we have our basic, most elemental being. Here we have our most

elemental contact. It is from the hypogastric plexus and the sacral ganglion that the dark forces of manhood and womanhood sparkle. From the dark plexus of sympathy run out the acute, intense sympathetic vibrations direct to the corresponding pole. Or so it should be in genuine passionate love. There is no mental interference. There is even no interference of the upper centres. Love is supposed to be blind. Though modern love wears strong spectacles.

.   .   .   .   .   .

(The consummation of sex) is the precise parallel of what happens in a thunderstorm.... There is a threefold result. First the flash of pure sensation and of real electricity. Then there is the birth of an entirely new state in each partner. And then there is the liberation. But the main thing, as in the thunderstorm, is the absolute renewal of the atmosphere: in this case, the blood.... And in this renewal lies the magic of sex.

All of which is very nearly true, but only very nearly. The mark is just missed and because of this the thought is invalidated.

I agree that "in sex we have our basic, most elemental being". But not because in sex the sensual or lower self is concerned and this alone, nor because this self is the real self of a man or a woman. When a man is really man, when he is whole and one, possessing the unity of an organism, not that of an aggregate, then there is neither a higher nor a lower self, but only one self, his self. So that if, as I believe, sex union means the bringing into contact of two selves and a consequent mutual fulfilment of these, they will be concerned in their full unity, not in part, but as wholes. Then, of course, there will be no mental interference as Lawrence says; but not because there is an unbridgeable gulf between body and mind, between the sensual self and the ideal self; rather, because these in the whole man do not exist apart, because, in a way, they do not exist at all, sinking and losing identity and separate existence in the unity of the whole. When man is truly man he is neither body, nor mind, nor even body *and* mind, but is just man, a unity, or as I prefer it, Spirit. And because of this I agree that love is blind, for what is meant by this is that in love there is no cognition. Only the mind knows cognitively and this cognitive knowledge is identified by philosophers and other divided men with that which they call real knowledge. Thus the philosophers would say that in love there is no knowledge at all: that is, that love is blind. In so far as there is none of their knowledge in love, in genuine love, I would agree. Of course, there is not, simply because there is a knowledge which transcends this knowledge, a knowledge which perhaps may be said to be wholly particular, a knowledge or coming into contact with another self. And about this knowledge there can be no thinking, for he who thinks (in the philosophical sense, of course) has never experienced this kind of knowing, because he is divided, his unity disintegrated. While he who has experienced this does not think philosophically, because such thinking is a substitute for living and he who is whole lives, having no need of a physician and a physician's substitutes for living.

I would agree too that there is a threefold result: "First the flash of pure sensation.... Then there is the birth of an entirely new state in each partner. And then there is the liberation". But the pure sensation is not a bodily sensation, a sensation in the usual meaning of the term, but a sensation of the whole individual, a sensation or feeling of the whole as Spirit, a spiritual orgasm, if you like. Neither is the birth of a new state in each partner the birth of a new bodily state, a renewal of the blood alone. Rather it is a creative renewal, reaffirmation, growth of the whole man, of the whole woman. And finally I would agree that there is liberation, a liberation of each individual from the essential loneliness which is the individual's by virtue of his individuality. But it is not as Lawrence thought a liberation only of the sensual self, from *its* loneliness or particularity. In so far as I am whole, an individual, I am one and isolated from other individuals. In coitus, complete, or, as I would call it, spiritual coitus, there is a liberation from that isolation, a transcendence of the loneliness which is mine because I am I. I become, and, therefore, am, more than myself. This truly is the magic and mystery of sex, magic because of the wonder of the creativity of it, mystery because it is nonsense to the cognitive mind and the philosophers. And the magic and mystery of it are the magic and mystery of Life which is beyond cognition.

Although Lawrence fell just short of the truth about sex, his attitude to it is of the greatest importance to-day. When we consider, what he saw more clearly than anyone, that the prevailing perversion and disease of our time is "sex in the head", we cannot fail to realise that this attitude of his was (and still is) a necessary step towards the recognition of that truth. Sex in the head!

> At present, sex is the mind's preoccupation, and in the body we
>   only mentally fornicate.
> To-day, we've got no sex.
> We have only cerebral excitations.
>
>   .   ∙   .   .   .   .
>
> The moment the mind interferes with love, or the will fixes on it,
> or the personality assumes it as an attribute, or the ego takes
>   possession of it,
> it isn't love any more, it's just a mess.
> And we've made a great mess of love, mind-perverted, will-
>   perverted, ego-perverted love.

Sex in the head! But that is not all. Worse there is still. There are the *mind-lifers* as Lawrence calls them. Like Clifford in *Lady Chatterley's Lover*, who symbolises them, they are paralysed from the waist downwards; they are either entirely impotent and are glad of it or else, what amounts to the same thing, they "have sex" as they "have a bath", more appropriately, as they "have a tooth out"—in order to keep their minds fit, their beloved little intellects up to the mark. So there must be a Resurrection of the Body! Says Dukes in *Lady Chatterley's Lover*:

> Give me the resurrection of the body! When we've shoved the
> cerebral stone away a bit, the money and the rest. Then we'll get
> a democracy of touch, instead of a democracy of pocket.

And Connie herself cries out at her husband's remark that he supposed a woman didn't take a supreme pleasure in the life of the mind:

Is that sort of idiocy the supreme pleasure of the life of the mind? No thank you! Give me the body. I believe the life of the body is a greater reality than the life of the mind: when the body is really awakened into life.

And then

The human body is only just coming to real life. With the Greeks it gave a lovely flicker, then Plato and Aristotle killed it, and Jesus finished it off. But now the body is really coming to life, is really rising from the tomb. And it will be a lovely, lovely life in the lovely universe, the life of the human body.

The Resurrection of the Body! Lawrence thought that that would put things right. In a way he was correct. But after the Resurrection of the Body there must and will be a Resurrection of Man, of Man the Spirit, who in being Man, in being Spirit, is more than Body and more than Mind. Somehow or other, although it is inconsistent with the rest of his thought, this seems to be what Lawrence was getting at in *The Plumed Serpent* and *The Man Who Died*. In the former Cipriano says:

> Man that is man is more than a man.
> No man is man till he is more than a man.

And in the latter, the Man Who Died, beneath the healing hands of the woman of Isis, feels:

I am going to be warm again, and I am going to be whole! I shall be warm like the morning. I shall be a man. It doesn't need understanding. It needs newness. She brings me newness——

It is the Resurrection of Man! The Risen Lord!

And the tragedy of it all is that Lawrence, who saw this, never realised it in himself, could never realise it. He, being Son of Woman, could never become Man. He remained always a man. *The Plumed Serpent* and *The Man Who Died* are wish-fulfilment books.

The opposition of Body to Mind, then, reduces to an opposition of the individual to the universal. Body is individual,

Mind universal. And this in turn to the opposition of Life to Death. Mind by universalising the individual destroys his individuality, destroys man's oneness, his manhood, in the end, his life. It mechanises, it gives laws, precepts, absolute goods and all the rest. It turns Man into a Machine. So man, if he is to be Man, if he wants to live, must fight the machine, must conquer it, for the machine is both symbolic and the instrument of the Intellect. In the end, Lawrence believes that he *will* conquer it.

> They talk of the triumph of the machine,
> but the machine will never triumph.

>   . . . at last
> all the creatures that cannot die while one heart harbours them
> they will hear a silence fall
> as the machines fail and finish;
> they will hear the faint rending of the asphalt roads
> as the hornbeam pushes up his sprouts;
> they will hear far, far away the last factory hooter
> send up the last wild cry of despair
> as the machine breaks finally down.

> And then at last
> all the creatures that were driven back into the uttermost corners
>   of the soul
> they will peep forth.

This belief is based upon no rational ground. Indeed it is based upon no grounds at all, for the existence of grounds implies rationality. The appeal against the machine cannot be based upon that which has produced the machine. If there is to be an appeal at all, it must be an appeal to the whole man. This the mind-lifers would call an irrational or emotional appeal and dismiss accordingly. But the whole man is beyond both rationality and irrationality, even as he is beyond both good and evil, although in some strange way this very *beyondness* is good.

Where then do we stand? What is the solution which Lawrence offered? Can we accept it? To the last question

I would answer yes, providing what he said be modified in the light of his own division. And what he said is this:

> Man that is man is more than a man.
> No man is man till he is more than a man.

What does this mean? It does not mean as Lawrence thought that man is by nature twofold, body and mind, and that the truer man is the sensual man, the bodily man. It means, I think, that man to be Man must be more than just this. He must be completely one, a unity beyond thought and action, a living Spirit. And in sex there comes a moment when he realises that he is more even than this, the moment when he realises that he is a vehicle, a vehicle of Life. But, it will be objected, how is this a solution? It doesn't decide between Christianity and Communism, for instance, as Mr Eliot would have us; in asserting that Man is and must be one, a unity of Spirit, it tells us nothing about that unity, and so nothing about my unity which interests me most; in short, it tells us nothing at all, it is sheer mysticism. I agree, it *is* mysticism. I agree too that it solves none of the "modern dilemmas". There is no need for it to do so. For if all men *were* Men there would be no such dilemmas. Become, therefore, Man and, becoming so, realise that you are more than a man, and that in those moments when you are most Man, you are a vehicle, a vehicle of the Lord of Life that is the Holy Ghost. Submit unto Him. In this is Salvation.

POSTSCRIPT: Since writing this essay, I have read Lawrence's *Last Poems*, and these have compelled me to re-read Lawrence entirely, with the result that I have now revised the opinions given here. But, believing the "Footnote" may still retain some value, I have not attempted to make any alterations in the text.

HENRY JAMES—AN ASPECT

IT is possible for an author's friends to know him too well. His books are hidden behind the façade of his public life, and his friends remember his conversations when they have forgotten his characters. It is a situation which by its irony appealed to Henry James. At the time of his own siege of London, he took note of Robert Browning, the veteran victor seen at every dinner table.

"I have never ceased to ask myself", James wrote, "in this particular loud, sound, normal hearty presence, all so assertive and so whole, all bristling with prompt responses and expected opinions and usual views....I never ceased, I say, to ask myself what lodgement, on such premises, the rich proud genius one adored could ever have contrived, what domestic commerce the subtlety that was its prime ornament and the world's wonder have enjoyed, under what shelter the obscurity that was its luckless drawback and the world's despair have flourished."

It is a double irony that James himself should have so disappeared behind the public life. There are times when those who met him at Grosvenor House, those who dined with him at Chelsea, even the favoured few who visited him at Rye, seem, while they have remembered his presence (that great bald brow, those soothing and reassuring gestures) and the curiosity of his conversation (the voice ponderously refining and refining on his meaning), to have forgotten his books. This, at any rate, is a possible explanation of Mr MacCarthy's statement in a delightful and deceptive essay on *The World of Henry James*: "The universe and religion are as completely excluded from his books as if he had been an eighteenth-century writer. The sky above his people, the earth beneath them, contain no mysteries for them", and in the same essay that the religious sense "is singularly absent from his work".

It would indeed be singular if the religious sense were

absent. Consider the father, the son of a Presbyterian and intended for the ministry, who travelling in England was possessed (during a nervous disorder) by the teaching of Swedenborg and devoted the rest of his life to writing theological books which no one read. His inspiration was the same as William Blake's and it was not less strong because its expression was chilled between the icy limits of Boston. It is difficult to believe that a child brought up by Henry James senior did not inherit a few of his father's perplexities if not his beliefs. Certainly he inherited a suspicion of organised religion, although that suspicion conflicted with his deepest instinct, his passion for Europe and tradition.

It is a platitude that in all his novels one is aware of James's deep love of age; not one generation had tended the lawns of his country houses, but centuries of taste had smoothed the grass and weathered the stone, "the warm, weary brickwork". This love of age and tradition, even without his love of Italy, was enough to draw him towards the Catholic Church as, in his own words, "the most impressive convention in all history". As early as 1869, in a letter from Rome, he noted its aesthetic appeal.

In St Peter's I stayed some time. It's even beyond its reputation. It was filled with foreign ecclesiastics—great armies encamped in prayer on the marble plains of its pavement—an inexhaustible physiognomical study. To crown my day, on my way home, I met his Holiness in person—driving in prodigious purple state—sitting dim within the shadows of his coach with two uplifted benedictory fingers—like some dusky Hindoo idol in the depths of its shrine....From the high tribune of a great chapel of St Peter's I have heard in the Papal choir a strange old man sing in a shrill unpleasant soprano. I've seen troops of little tortured neophytes clad in scarlet, marching and counter-marching and ducking and flopping, like poor little raw recruits for the heavenly host.

But no one can long fail to discover how superficial is the purely aesthetic appeal of Catholicism; it is more accidental than the closeness of turf. The pageantry may be well done and excite the cultured visitor or it may be ill done and repel him. The Catholic Church has never hesitated to indulge in

the lowest forms of popular "art"; it has never used beauty
for the sake of beauty. Any little junk shop of statues and holy
pictures beside a cathedral is an example of what I mean.
"The Catholic Church, as churches go to-day," James wrote
in *A Little Tour in France*, "is certainly the most spectacular;
but it must feel that it has a great fund of impressiveness to
draw upon when it opens such sordid little shops of sanctity as
this." If it had been true that Henry James had no religious
sense and that Catholicism spoke only to his aesthetic sense,
Catholicism and Henry James at this point would finally have
parted company; or if his religious sense had been sufficiently
vague and "numinous", he would then surely have ap-
proached the Anglican Church to discover whether he could
find there satisfaction for the sense of awe and reverence,
whether he could build within it his system of "make-believe".
If the Anglican Church did not offer to his love of age so unbroken a tradition, it offered to an Englishman or an American
a purer literary appeal. Crashaw's style, if it occasionally has
the beauty of those "marble plains", is more often the poetical
equivalent of the shop for holy statues; it has neither the purity
nor the emotional integrity of Herbert's and Vaughan's; nor
as literature can the Douai Bible be compared with the
Authorised Version. And yet the Anglican Church never
gained the least hold on James's interest, while the Catholic
Church seems to have retained its appeal to the end. He
never even felt the possibility of choice: it was membership
of the Catholic Church or nothing. Rowland Mallet wondered "whether it be that one tacitly concedes to the Roman
Church the monopoly of a guarantee of immortality, so that
if one is indisposed to bargain with her for the precious gift
one must do without it altogether".

In James's first novel, *Roderick Hudson*, published in 1875,
six years after his first sight of the high tribune and the
tortured neophytes, the hero "pushed into St Peter's, in whose
vast clear element the hardest particles of thought ever in-
fallibly entered into solution. From a heartache to a Roman

rain there were few contrarieties the great church did not help
him to forget". The same emotion was later expressed in
novel after novel. In times of mental weariness, at moments
of crisis, his characters inevitably find their way into some
dim nave, to some lit altar; Merton Densher, haunted by his
own treachery, enters the Brompton Oratory, "on the edge
of a splendid service—the flocking crowd told of it—which
glittered and resounded, from distant depths, in the blaze of
altar lights and the swell of organ and choir. It didn't match
his own day, but it was much less of a discord than some
other things actual and possible".

It is a rather lukewarm tribute to a religious system, but
Strether in *The Ambassadors*, published in 1903, enters Notre-
Dame for a more significant purpose.

He was aware of having no errand in such a place but the desire
not to be, for the hour, in certain other places; a sense of safety, of
simplification, which each time he yielded to it he amused himself
by thinking of as a private concession to cowardice. The great
church had no altar for his worship, no direct voice for his soul;
but it was none the less soothing even to sanctity; for he could feel
while there what he couldn't elsewhere, that he was a plain tired
man taking the holiday he had earned. He was tired, but he
wasn't plain—that was the pity and the trouble of it; he was able,
however, to drop his problem at the door very much as if it had
been the copper piece that he deposited, on the threshold, in the
receptacle of the inveterate blind beggar. He trod the long dim
nave, sat in the splendid choir, paused before the clustered chapels
of the east end, and the mighty monument laid upon him its spell.
. . . This form of sacrifice did at any rate for the occasion as well as
another; it made him quite sufficiently understand how, within
the precinct, for the real refugee, the things of the world could fall
into abeyance. That was the cowardice, probably—to dodge them,
to beg the question, not to deal with it in the hard outer light; but
his own oblivions were too brief, too vain, to hurt anyone but himself, and he had a vague and fanciful kindness for certain persons
whom he met, figures of mystery and anxiety, and whom, with
observation for his pastime, he ranked with those who were fleeing
from justice. Justice was outside, in the hard light, and injustice
too; but one was as absent as the other from the air of the long
aisles and the brightness of the many altars.

It is worth noting, in connexion with Mr MacCarthy's criticism, that this was not Strether's first visit to Notre-Dame:

he had lately made the pilgrimage more than once by himself —had quite stolen off, taking an unnoticed chance and making no point of speaking of the adventure when restored to his friends.

In 1875 Rowland Mallet found in St Peter's relief for most contrarieties "from a heartache to a Roman rain"; in 1903 Strether found in Notre-Dame "a sense of safety, of simplification"; the difference is remarkably small, and almost equally small the difference between Strether's feelings and those of the "real refugee", whom he watched "from a respectable distance, remarking some note of behaviour, of penitence, of prostration, of the absolved, relieved state". Strether wondered whether the attitude of a woman who sat without praying "were some congruous fruit of absolution, of 'indulgence'. He knew but dimly what indulgence, in such a place, might mean; yet he had, as with a soft sweep, a vision of how it might indeed add to the zest of active rights". It would have been a more astonishing avowal if Strether's knowledge had been less dim, and it must be admitted that the vagueness of James's knowledge, which led him sometimes ludicrously astray, may have contributed to the emotional appeal.

But it would be unfair to attribute this constant intrusion of the Catholic Church merely to the unreasoning emotions. There were dogmas in Catholic teaching, avoided by the Anglican Church, which attracted James, and one of these dealt with prayers for the dead.

Mr MacCarthy mentions James's horror of "the brutality and rushing confusion of the world, where the dead are forgotten", and James himself, trying to trace the genesis of that beautiful and ridiculous story *The Altar of the Dead*, came to the conclusion that the idea embodied in it "had always, or from ever so far back, been there". This is not to say that he was conscious of how fully Catholic teaching might have satisfied

his desire not merely to commemorate but to share life with
the dead. Commemoration—there is as much acreage of
marble monument in the London churches as any man can
need; James wanted something more living, something sym-
bolised in his mind, in the story to which I refer, by candles
on an altar. It was not exactly prayer, but how close it was
to prayer, how near James was to believing that the dead
have need of prayer, may be seen in the case of George
Stransom.

He had perhaps not had more losses than most men, but he had
counted his losses more; he hadn't seen death more closely, but
had in a manner felt it more deeply. He had formed little by little
the habit of numbering his Dead: it had come to him early in life
that there was something one had to do for them. They were there
in their simplified intensified essence, their conscious absence and
expressive patience, as personally there as if they had only been
stricken dumb. When all sense of them failed, all sound of them
ceased, it was as if their purgatory were really still on earth: they
asked so little that they got, poor things, even less, and died again,
died every day, of the hard usage of life. They had no organised
service, no reserved place, no honour, no shelter, no safety.

The Altar of the Dead I have called ridiculous as well as
beautiful, and it is ridiculous because James never understood
that his desire to help the dead was not a personal passion,
that it did not require secret subjective rites. Haunted by this
idea of the neglected dead, "the general black truth that
London was a terrible place to die in", by the phrase of his
foreign friend, as they watched a funeral train "bound merrily
by" on its way to Kensal Green, "Mourir à Londres, c'est
être bien mort", James was literally driven into a church.
Stransom leaves the grey foggy afternoon for "a temple of
the old persuasion, and there had evidently been a function—
perhaps a service for the dead; the high altar was still a blaze
of candles. This was an exhibition he always liked, and he
dropped into a seat with relief. More than it had ever yet
come home to him it struck him as good there should be
churches". This one might expect to be the end of Stransom's

search. He had only to kneel, to pray, to remember. But again the subjective beauty of the story is caricatured by the objective action. Stransom buys an altar for one of the chapels: "the altar and the sacred shell that half encircled it, consecrated to an ostensible and customary worship, were to be splendidly maintained; all that Stransom reserved to himself was the number of his lights and the free enjoyment of his intentions". Surely no one so near in spirit, at any rate in this one particular, to the Catholic Church was ever so ignorant of its rules. How was it that a writer as careful as James to secure the fullest authenticity for his subjects could mar in this way one of his most important stories? It cannot be said that he had not the time to study Catholicism; there was no limit to the time which James would devote to anything remotely connected with his art. Was it perhaps that the son of the old Swedenborgian was afraid of capture? A friend of James once spoke to him of a lady who had been converted to Catholicism. James was silent for a long while; then he remarked that he envied her.

The second point which may have attracted James to the Church was its treatment of supernatural evil. The Anglican Church had almost relinquished Hell. It smoked and burned on Sundays only in obscure provincial pulpits, but no day passed in a Catholic Church without prayers for deliverance from evil spirits "wandering through the world for the ruin of souls". This savage elementary belief found an echo in James's sophisticated mind, to which the evil of the world was very present. He faced it in his work with a religious intensity. The man was sensitive, a lover of privacy, but it is absurd for Mr MacCarthy to picture the writer "flying with frightened eyes and stopped ears from that City of Destruction till the terrified bang of his sanctuary door leaves him palpitating but safe".

If he fled from London to Rye, it was the better to turn at bay. This imaginary world, which according to Mr Mac-Carthy he created, peopled with "beings who had leisure and

the finest faculties for comprehending and appreciating each
other, where the reward of goodness was the recognition of
its beauty", comes not from James's imagination but from
Mr MacCarthy's; the world of Henry James's novels is a
world of treachery and deceit, of Gilbert Osmund and Madame
Merle, of Kate Croy and Merton Densher, of Catherine Stant
and the Prince, of Bloodgood, of Madame de Vionnet; a
realist's world in which Osmund is victorious, Isabel Archer
defeated, Densher gains his end and Millie Theale dies disillusioned. The novels are only saved from the deepest cynicism by the religious sense; the struggle between the beautiful
and the treacherous is lent, as in Hardy's novels, the importance of the supernatural, human nature is not despicable
in Osmund or Densher, for they are both capable of damnation. "It is true to say", Mr Eliot has written in an essay on
Baudelaire, "that the glory of man is his capacity for salvation; it is also true to say that his glory is his capacity for
damnation. The worst that can be said of most of our male-
factors, from statesmen to thieves, is that they are not men
enough to be damned". This worst cannot be said of James's
characters: both Densher and the Prince have on their faces
the flush of the flames.

One remembers in this context the poor damned ghost of
Brydon's other self, Brydon, the American expatriate and
cultured failure, who returns after many years and in his New
York house becomes aware of another presence, the self he
might have been, unhappy and ravaged with a million a year
and ruined sight and crippled hand. Through the great house
he hunts the ghost, until it turns at bay under the fanlight in
the entrance hall.

Rigid and conscious, spectral yet human, a man of his own substance and stature waited there to measure himself with his power
to dismay. This only could it be—this only till he recognised, with
his advance, that what made the face dim was the pair of raised
hands that covered it and in which, so far from being offered in
defiance, it was buried as for dark deprecation. So Brydon, before
him, took him in; with every fact of him now, in the higher light,

hard and acute—his planted stillness, his vivid truth, his grizzled bent head and white masking hands, his queer actuality of evening dress, of dangling double eyeglass, of gleaming silk lappet and white linen, of pearl button and gold watch-guard and polished shoe.... He could but gape at his other self in this other anguish, gape as a proof that *he*, standing there for the achieved, the enjoyed, the triumphant life, couldn't be faced in his triumph. Wasn't the proof in the splendid covering hands, strong and completely spread?—so spread and so intentional that, in spite of a special verity that surpassed every other, the fact that one of these hands had lost two fingers, which were reduced to stumps, as if accidentally shot away, the face was effectually guarded and saved.

When the hands drop they disclose a face of horror, evil, odious, blatant, vulgar, and as the ghost advances, Brydon falls back "as under the hot breath and the roused passion of a life larger than his own, a rage of personality before which his own collapsed".

The story has been quoted by an American critic as an example of the fascination and repulsion James felt for his country. The idea that he should have stayed and faced his native scene never left him; he never ceased to wonder whether he had not cut himself off from the source of deepest inspiration. This the story reveals on one level of consciousness; on a deeper level it is not too fanciful to see in it an expression of faith in man's ability to damn himself. A rage of personality—it is a quality of the religious sense, a spiritual quality which the materialist writer can never convey, not even Dickens, by the most adept use of exaggeration.

It is tempting to reinforce this point—James's belief in supernatural evil—with *The Turn of the Screw*. Here in the two evil spirits—Peter Quint, the dead valet, with his ginger hair and his little whiskers and his air of an actor and "his white face of damnation", and Miss Jessel "dark as midnight in her black dress, her haggard beauty and her unutterable woe"—is the explicit breath of Hell. They declare themselves in every attitude and glance, with everything but voice, to be suffering the torments of the damned, the torments which they intend the two children to share. It is tempting to point to the scene of Miles's confession which frees him from the possession of Peter Quint. But James himself has uttered too clear a warning. The story is, in his words, "a fairy tale pure and simple", something seasonable for Christmas, "a piece of ingenuity pure and simple, of cold artistic calculation, an *amusette* to catch those not easily caught ..., the jaded, the disillusioned, the fastidious". So a valuable ally must be relinquished, not without a mental reservation that no one by mere calculation could have made the situation so "reek with the air of Evil" and amazement that such a story should have been thought seasonable for Christmas.

Hell and Purgatory, James came very close to a direct statement of his belief in both of these. What personal experience of treachery and death stood between the author of *Washington Square* and *The Bostonians* and the author of *The Wings of a Dove* and *The Golden Bowl* is not known. The younger author might have developed into the gentle, urbane social critic of Mr MacCarthy's imagination, the later writer is only just prevented from being as explicitly religious as Dostoievski by the fact that neither a philosophy nor a creed ever emerged from his religious sense. His religion was always a mirror of his experience. Experience taught him to believe in supernatural evil, but not in supernatural good. Millie Theale is all human; her courage has not the supernatural support which holds Kate Croy and Catherine Stant in a strong coil. The rage of personality is all the devil's. The good and the beautiful meet betrayal with patience and forgiveness, but without sublimity, and their death is at best a guarantee of no more pain. Ralph Touchett dying at Gardencourt only offers himself the consolation that pain is passing. "I don't know why we should suffer so much. Perhaps I shall find out."

It would be wrong to leave the impression that James's religious sense ever brought him nearer than hailing distance to an organised system, even to a system organised by himself. The organising ability exhausted itself in his father and elder brother. James never tried to state a philosophy, and this reluctance to trespass outside his art may have led Mr MacCarthy astray. But no one, with the example of Hardy before them, can deny that James was right. The novelist depends preponderantly on his personal experience, the philosopher on correlating the experience of others, and the novelist's philosophy will always be a little lop-sided. There is much in common between the pessimism of Hardy and of James; both had a stronger belief in supernatural evil than in supernatural good, and if James had, like Hardy, tried to systematise his ideas, his novels too would have lurched with the same one-sided gait. They retain their beautiful symmetry at a price, the price which Turgenev paid and Dostoievski refused to pay, the price of refraining from adding to the novelist's distinction that of a philosopher or a religious teacher of the second rank.

ANGER AGAINST BOOKS

OR should it be, anger against reviewing? Reviewing is an ill-paid trade, not in relation to the amount of work one does, for that—once the reviewing technique is mastered—is not large, nor strenuous, but in relation to the amount of corrosion which one's mind is bound to suffer in the course of considering, however lightly and professionally, all these piles of printed words. Or should it be anger against seeing the stuff lying about, books on chairs and tables and floor, a kind of flood that neither magic nor a good housemaid can deal with? Even the table where I work is covered with obscene little embryos—bits of paper with words scrawled on them, which I know from experience are going sooner or later to turn into another of these cloth-bound objects which are constantly bursting out of the shelves on to the top of me. Oh horrible, this nice clean piece of paper that I slid tidily under the platen of my typewriter just a few minutes ago, it is rapidly becoming covered with words; there is a plot between it and the red note-book which my son treacherously gave me for Christmas, and which must have cost him at least a shilling, a liaison between them to produce at least part of another book.

It is all very alarming. It is alarming enough to think of the time yesterday when the pencil notes were getting written into the red note-book, and the time when the clean sheet of typing paper was picked up and put into the jaws of the typewriter (which is a time so near at hand that it is very nearly now), and the time whose tail I only just failed to hold when I started thinking this sentence, and—and "now"—"now" escaping as I write it—"now" that *you*, in the future, *you*, at the moment (because *you* are certainly in the present, aren't you?), will either think of as your immediately occurring now,

or else as the past when I was (or do I mean I am?) writing
this, according to your temperament—there, I've let go of the
thing's tail and it has gone chasing back into the past! And
the present that you, reading, are in, which is future by several
months, perhaps by several years, from here, is curiously solid
and real to me. I can see you. I can think of the feel of the
book in your hand, I can get behind your eye and half
notice, as you are noticing, the length of line, the margin, the
palish shape of the thumb on the edge of the book. I can very
nearly remember it, as though it were as much part of the
past to me now as I writing will be part of the past to you
reading. And supposing I have died between now and then
(or, if you like, between then and now), that makes no difference to the solidity of the future you to the present me.

Things which one can't properly understand are frightening, and frightening things make one angry. And this time
business is always cropping up. There seems to be no evidence
that it bothered one's ancestors much when they wrote.
Perhaps one of the special reasons for its importance now is
that our lives and circumstances are changing so rapidly that
we cannot but be conscious of time. It is no longer a sober
progression from cradle to grave, a thing so calm and ritual
that it is not really frightening. It is not a soft, an ever-rolling
stream; on the contrary, it is something which is liable to
bump one over precipices at any moment, to change everything one does and hopes and thinks. One is always in the
awkward position of suddenly finding one has turned into
somebody else, with different interests, a different inner life,
though—oddly enough—the same, or practically the same,
outside to look at and see with, and the same immediate
human relationships and, unfortunately, the same up-bring-
ing, the same set of chromosomes and the same social biases.

The worst of writing about time is that it is very difficult to
stop. In writing down that "now" two paragraphs old which
has become irrevocable past for both you and me (much more
so for me, because all this takes longer to write than to read)

I had merely meant to point out its alarmingness and then go on to certain other alarming things about the making, and for that matter the reading—for both writer and reader go to a completed whole—of books. Let me skip off this moving staircase while I see a chance, and light safely on a small but, to the best of my belief, stable pile of statistics.

During the last three years an average of about fifteen thousand books have been published in this country. These can be subdivided, and the yearly average works out at, for instance, 4332 novels, 588 books of poetry and drama (which for some reason are lumped together—I suppose they will include about a dozen books containing something approaching real poetry, and perhaps rather more goodish plays), and 808 books on economics and politics—their number went up considerably last year. There are always a vast number of devotional and children's books, but as these are generally printed on worse paper, they have an engaging habit of disappearing from the world, dissipating themselves into dust and tatters, with a reasonable rapidity.

Even in the matter of material it is rather horrid to think about. Once there were pine forests—you know the air there is in pine forests, either sun-warmed when all the sweetness comes out of it, so that one can shut one's eyes and stand breathing and floating and tingling, or else cold and resiny, reflected back perhaps from snow, so that one raises one's head and feels it sweeping through lungs and body. Well, that's all gone into the books, which do not smell nice at all. And then there were miles of esparto grass, which is not very pretty, but was at least alive and green and impersonal. Or there were rags, properly cleaned and sorted but rather odd-looking all the same, rather intimately connected with real life. And there was chalk, which our earliest forbears knew as the stuff you found flints for arrow-heads in. There were various other materials, besides the binding and not to speak of the ink. It has all turned into books. It might have turned into something else, something beautiful or something to wear

or something to do with houses or ships or tools; the chalk
might have turned into tooth powder; the forest might have
turned into more forests, for thousands and thousands of
years. But it did turn into books. Why? What is the good of
books anyway, above all, so many books?

Books, like other things, have a cash basis. The middlemen,
naturally, do well out of them; not so well this year as they
have in earlier years, but probably well enough. Some of
them distribute the books, and this is, in some ways, a rather
more complicated business than distributing tinned salmon,
though perhaps not so complicated as distributing motor-
cars or Paris hats. Others publish and advertise the books,
and this also is a complicated business, more complicated in
many ways than running an ordinary small factory, not to
speak of a poultry farm or a nursery garden—though these
two need more brains than one might think—but not so complicated as making and advertising either an expensive educational system, or gas-bombs and submarines. At any rate,
the middlemen are driven by economic necessity, even though
some of them have other motives as well. Oddly enough, it is
not usually thought very reputable for a publisher—or even
a bookseller—to have non-economic motives. A publisher
does not like to be thought of as having religious, political, or
even markedly aesthetic tastes; he prefers that one should
consider him simply as a business man. It improves his
economic position.

And the authors? They, of course, are driven by economic
motives too. But not quite in the way that they think they
are. Although in any gathering of authors, there is constant
and eager discussion of royalties, percentages, sales and so
forth, this is mostly rather naïve; they are talking about these
things because they, like the publishers, want to be thought
of as business men and women; they are very anxious that the
world—and the other authors—should realise how grown-up
they really are, that their mothers came from Aberdeen and
their fathers from Jerusalem. But this is not the whole of the

story. Very few of them are writing with an immediate eye on royalties, and if they do they often miss them. But what has happened is that the authors have been brought up and educated in a certain way, implying a certain amount of money, and now they are living in a way which implies the existence of surplus money, not only owned by the people who buy the books, but by the authors and their friends. It is a little crude to say that they write this way or that way because their economic circumstances are this or that. But consider in practice the things that the possession of money does to authors. Think of D. H. Lawrence, from the time he first got out of the working classes (he didn't write till he *was* out), the changes that his and other people's money made in his books. Think of Shaw. Think of Galsworthy. Think of all the men and women who have somehow or another got together enough money to buy themselves leisure to use for writing!

Or take it another way. Say what the Victorians—or the Greeks—might have said. Say that the breath of God blows through us. But we are the kind of instrument that we are because of the way we live. We can't get away from ourselves; we can't become pure impersonal machines; we can't be objective, outside ourselves. We are the flutes of Apollo and we are made of a certain wood to start with. And the wood is what we grew into, because of the seed, because of the soil, because of the amount of sunlight or rain that helped or hindered our growth. It is extremely annoying not to be able to change the wood we are made of; we can become better technically; the instrument can be scraped and smoothed, pierced with sharp pains or oiled from the olives of flattery. And we can observe the other kind of wood, we can see the difference in grain and colour, count the rings of growth; but we can never become it, however much we want to.

These are our limitations. With this kind of equipment we write books. Given that we can't get away from ourselves, our environment, and our historical period, we try, on the whole, to do two things. We try to put before people some idea or ideas which appear to us to be important, and we try to tell a story. Now, by "telling a story" I don't mean only writing a novel or a tale or a narrative poem; I mean putting down something in a connected and interesting way so that one part leads on from another; a good argument on any subject is essentially a story—one follows it in the same way. A poem is a story in so far as one line makes one want to read the next; some continuous process is made to happen in the mind of the reader, and when any book is dull, it is usually that this story-making faculty is dim in the writer.

We all, I think, want to be read: we may imagine the audience as a very small one; certain writers—say James Joyce on the one hand or a pure mathematician on the other —have a very limited audience which can possibly hope to understand them. This limited audience is usually of tech-nicians, and has the merit that its attention is more con-centrated than an ordinary lay audience. Other writers write for a general audience and also for a limited audience. Perhaps most high-brow authors do that. I, for instance, write for a general audience, but when I am writing historical novels I also, and perhaps most intently, write for an audience of historians and archaeologists, who alone can see some of my fine points. This special audience comprises perhaps a few hundred English-speaking men and women, of whom perhaps a dozen or so will read the book or see the points which so pleased me when I was carefully making them. But without this dozen, the thing which I write is incomplete.

Yet possibly it will not reach them at all. Again, as the years pass, another kind of idea one has wanted to express, which one has expressed in certain sentences, will become unintelligible to all except a more and more limited audience of people with a historical sense. For instance, in my first book, *The Conquered*, no one will really get what I meant them to get out of it unless he or she remembers the political and emotional situation between Ireland and England from 1916 to 1921. This fact of the incompleteness of the book without the right audience is one of the things which is so heart-breaking about being a writer, or indeed a reader, for we are too often conscious of our deficiencies as audience, though again there are moments when we feel we are the one, essential, chosen audience, for whom it was all written. But then—what does the writer say to that?

Obviously, a good many of the younger authors write for a very personal audience. But the better they get the more the circle widens. It seems possible that this personal-audience habit is one which is contracted at the Universities, especially perhaps at Oxford, where the personal audience happens as naturally as it did in Athens. But when the personal audience ceases to seem natural, a good author will drop the concept of it, and not try—as some of them have—to bring it over into some convenient quarter of London, or even Paris.

We write, then, for our readers. But what if our readers do not understand us? Certainly most of them won't. Not completely, that is. Is it better for those who practise the other arts? Sometimes we think so. We say to ourselves, the painter puts down exactly what he wants the onlooker to see, so that colour and shape can't be muddled or misunderstood. Blue is not only blue, but an utterly exact shade of blue (supposing, as I think we reasonably can, that only a few of the observers have any ocular abnormality); this curve runs definitely into that. It is all set down.

But here we come across difficulties at once. It is obviously harder for the painter to get his work of art to its audience. It is more expensive than a book, and, worse still, there is only one of it. The chances are that only a very few people will see it. Of course, it is possible that it will be seen—and even bought—by the perfect and essential onlooker, who, seeing it, will complete it as a thing. But this is unlikely. Few pictures get much seen until after their artists' deaths, and then presumably the historical sense is needed among the onlookers to complete the contact. That is not very satisfactory. And again, it is startling to find the many different reactions which any hundred onlookers, chosen at random, will have to almost any picture, including those which you or I feel to be definitely and incontrovertibly great art.

Perhaps architecture is more satisfactory. Here at least there is no lack of onlookers. Of the hundreds or thousands who pass and observe any building, some must appreciate it completely. But yet that isn't good enough. For a building is three-dimensional and, what is more, it is usually a tool. It is the people who use it that matter, though, oddly enough, architects do not always seem to realise this. It is the users of the building (for instance, the priests and congregation of an ancient temple or mediaeval church, the sellers and buyers in most large modern buildings) who must finally be the audience. And they are not always very good at noticing it, at any rate as a whole; very often, in fact, they have no opportunity of experiencing it as a whole. And even so we have to modify our statement, because modern buildings are also used as advertisements, and to some extent it is the potential buyers of goods who must be the judges. So architecture is not really very satisfactory either.

Suppose, now, I were to try another angle of approach. For I am trying to see what it is that makes one so angry with books. Can it perhaps have something to do with the fact that most modern books seem to have been written in and for and about the capitals of the world? I am taking capitals in a rather special sense. The greater London, in whose aura most English novels, books on politics and economics, biographies, etc., appear to have been written—and can that have anything to do with the fact that most publishing firms live within a few miles of one another and of Piccadilly Circus?—seems to miss out Kennington, Wapping, Balham and such places, but to include Oxford and Cambridge (in each of which there is at least one large firm of publishers). It takes, of course, a shorter time to get by ordinary methods of transport from Kensington or Bloomsbury to Oxford than, say, to Woolwich or Barking. There is something a little unreal about capitals.

They seem to contain the heads of everything and the life of nothing. Here in London, for instance, are the headquarters of all the political parties, but the *polis* is elsewhere, is dispersed.

In London we are both safer and more unsafe. Normally, the streets are clean and well lighted, communications are extraordinarily good; epidemics are kept firmly in check. Nothing unexpected happens; it is the world of Mrs Dalloway. At the same time, everything is so centralised that, for instance, a really efficient strike in two or three trades would cut communications, lighting, cooking and sanitation. And it would be beyond the power of an ordinary householder to put them together in the least. Few of us have more than a dozen candles in our houses; if we cook by gas, as an increasing number of households of all classes do, there is probably no fire upon which we could so much as boil a kettle properly, even if we have fuel. If water were cut off, there are hardly any springs or wells in the whole of London; most houses are miles distant from any open river, and most river water would have to be boiled or heavily treated with chloride of lime; very few houses near the centre of London have enough garden to allow of even moderately antiseptic earth pits, supposing our w.c.'s ceased to function. Such of us as have private means of transport, supposing the public means were cut off, depend upon a fresh supply of petrol to-morrow, and few households have stores enough to last them more than a week at most. Add to this that in any future war it seems probable that the capital cities of the countries engaged in war will probably be destroyed within a few hours. Along what a conditional, what a trembling precipice, is Mrs Dalloway walking!

Oxford and Cambridge are not quite in the same position, but they are in another sort of danger, which is, indeed, not absent from London. In these towns it becomes increasingly attractive to run away, to make for oneself—often with great labour and erudition—an academic system of values and

standards, in learning, morals and aesthetics. This system of
course is carried into practice in living as a social and
political being. And those who have the greatest influence in
the university communities are usually those who have these
standards most strongly, and can advance the most powerful
arguments on their behalf. And because one has been oneself
so much entangled in the same net, it is not always easy to
recognise a book produced in the London-Oxford-Cambridge
triangle for the awful nonsense that it so often is.

Yet sometimes a revelation of this kind comes to one suddenly in the middle of reviewing. One has, say, a batch of
perfectly good novels—from the point of view of the capital.
One inspects them for technique. One judges their emotional
effect, and the way they tell a story. And then suddenly one
thinks, what on earth is this about? And for a time one is
quite incapable of doing what one is going to be paid for and
writing an intelligent review. Sometimes this happens when
a book crops up which was not written from the safe point of
view, which does not come from a capital, but which is yet a
sufficiently good story to carry one completely through to a new
world. The difficulty is, that the capitals do seem to act as
focusing centres, and that some equally sharp focus is needed
to produce the same tenseness of creation. The most obvious
present foci seem to be the anti-capital nationalist centres.
Liam O'Flaherty and perhaps Neil Gunn, among novelists,
seem to have got away, and so do one or two of the writers,
like Henry Williamson, whom one might describe as English
nationalists.

There should, of course, be other foci, and perhaps there
are, but so far no adequate story-teller has come from them.
History, economics and politics all seem to come from the
triangle too. If Edinburgh became again an adequate
Scottish capital, there would probably be an Edinburgh-
Glasgow focus. Paris focuses. Berlin focuses. New York
focuses, or perhaps in America the focus is somewhere along
the eastern coast-line, including several pseudo-capitals. It

is too early yet to tell whether Moscow will become a focus too. But London, Paris and New York are the most typical, because the safest, capitals. It would be interesting to see what would happen if some of the publishing firms, and the headquarters of some of the newspapers, especially the weeklies, were to move out into the provinces.

So here one is, angry with the unreal, with the deliberately misleading, life of the capitals, reflected into books. Was it always like that? Look at the past, at the other bindings on the shelf. Yes, look at Athens! Look at Rome. Look at Florence. Look at St Petersburg—for that was its name then. Look at Paris, even more a capital *dans le temps perdu*. Look, for that matter, at Elizabethan London, holding in its mind yet other capitals—a tinier London, Rome, Alexandria, Elsinore. Those are the books which, more than any other books, helped to make one what one so distressingly is.

We have read too much. Book stuff comes between us and life. We are reading the whole time. Probably most of the printed matter which comes from the various presses of the world at this moment is advertisement. A good deal of it slides off us, leaving only the faintest sediment. But what about all these good books, the books one was encouraged to read—the books one has been made to take seriously? What have they done to us?

Quite certainly, these books have put certain ideas into our minds, hammering them in with vivid images, with beautiful words. They have put into our heads, for instance, certain very definite ideas about private property in things and persons, about love and hate and jealousy, certain very definite values which were the values of the person writing the book and which he has made by story-telling to seem permanent. These old ideas which were fortunate enough to find a vehicle of words, to be put into us by the story of Romeo and Juliet or King Lear or Oedipus, or whatever it may have been, are strong and tough in our minds. If we want to fight them they defend themselves with glorious and moving words. They walk in music. It is very hard for us to clothe our new, our half-made ideas in stories that are as good as the old ones. The best we can often do is to undermine the old stories by criticism or laughter. We can try to stop their being read in schools, but that is rather difficult. And we can examine our own consciences or imaginations about them.

It is very interesting to notice how full of book images we are, how certain quotations come up to the surface of our minds at the least provocation. If our loves are kind we feel for them in terms of mediaeval or even Victorian lyricists, if they are difficult in terms of John Donne, if they are really very annoying in terms of Ovid or Catullus. We are always the gentleman with Shakespeare or Aeschylus, and, if we want to express dissatisfaction, there is our Eliot in his appropriate corner. It is depressing to feel that "Oh! western wind" has been written once for all, and that it was not we ourselves who wrote it. It is depressing to think of how many combinations of words have been used. Which book shall I write? Which indeed!

Try to do anything, experience anything, take any kind of action. Can you possibly do it without book associations? Can you be free from any relationship with heroes and heroines, or indeed villains and villainesses? Can you think of yourself in terms which are not book-soiled? I doubt it. We are all, unhappily, educated, and it has been, more than perhaps we realise, a book education. We have been taught to respect books. One awful result of that is that we grow up to respect newspapers, and even to respect printed advertisements. And we cannot get over the fact of that average fifteen thousand titles, many of which must have sold a good many thousand copies. What is to be done about it?

There are two lines in one of Auden's last poems, from an extremely beautiful description of a possible kind of Good Life:

> All of the women and most of the men
> Shall work with their hands and not think again.

Now, reading printed matter does not necessarily mean thought; but still, a good many books do require a certain amount of cerebral agitation from the reader. And the tendency everywhere is to make us think more. In Russia a few years ago there were large districts where the perfection which Auden aims at in his poem definitely existed. Everyone worked with their hands—and their arms and legs and bodies, so that the whole thing wore out very rapidly after the age of forty or so (probably younger for the average child-bearing woman). But now this idyllic state has changed. The peasants are being violently and constantly educated; schools are being put up everywhere; men and woman alike find it very difficult to keep out of being taught to read. And the reading is not for pleasure or day-dreaming; no, the object, I am afraid, is to make them think. Presumably the proportions of published books would be very different in Russia. There would be many fewer novels and immensely more books about economics, and technical books of all kinds, the sort of book one can't get through a page of without doing a little thinking. Books are relatively cheap; they are one of the few things beyond immediate necessities that people do ordinarily buy. There are book shops and book stalls in all towns, and men and women, boys and girls, go about their business, walking or tramming, and reading the most serious-looking books as if they were really enjoying them.

This is the tendency in the U.S.S.R., and in all countries the same thing is happening on a smaller scale: those who have not had education in the past are clamouring for it now, and there is always a body of educated people who are clamorously eager to give it to them. They are potential book-readers. They are going to demand mind-fodder. They will do this particularly if the alternative is not "work with their hands" but the increasingly usual alternative in most countries of standing about with nothing to do and no particular hope of anything to do in the future. Even crime cannot occupy more than a certain percentage of the population and there are some people who definitely find it uncongenial. There are, of course, certain other alternatives, but, as this is not a political essay (except in so far as everything one writes is coloured by one's position in the community and one's hopes for it), I had better not talk about that. In any case, it is apt to mean a certain outpouring of the printed word too; there are probably not even enough cheap second-hand editions of Marx to go round.

What, then, are we writers doing about this? We are aware of it, we are bothered, we are even angry. We are angry because we feel so intensely our own inadequacy. Of course we don't always say that's it, because one must after all keep up the dignity of the dear old profession, and besides, some of us are making so much money that we are bound to feel that we are doing a Good Thing already, so we at least needn't bother our heads. But it is apparent. Our works give us away. We fret and fidget and howl aloud our perplexities; we are one of the few sets of people who can give themselves the pleasure of letting go—of lying on the floor and drumming on it with our spiritual heels, squealing for our Freudian nannies, and generally throwing ourselves about with the jolly certainty that someone will pay for the privilege of watching us.

Some of us definitely turn and run. We become for instance Catholics, or Fascists, or something similar in which we can give up our perplexities and worries and angers and take refuge on some maternal bosom. Some of us find a different kind of refuge, an increasingly deep and tortuous bore-hole into the problems of the separate individual. This is certainly more interesting, and it takes a good deal of energy to be the kind of grub which bores its tunnels through the solid oak of centuries of upbringing and tradition and taboo; but one does tend to lose sight of the daylight and never to be able to get back into it. And that is rather awkward sooner or later, especially if one suddenly becomes angry or annoyed with the narrowness of one's tunnel.

A few of us have a sufficiently interesting life not to need to run away. Stella Benson, I take it, is sufficiently occupied in coping with wars, famines, bandits and other normal distractions of the Chinese householder to have to consider any merely spiritual escape. Women writers with children can, with any luck, count on the measles to take their minds off the problems of abstract value. Some youngish men writers, especially, perhaps, those who had a year or so, but not more, of the war, find almost any kind of violent action pleasantly satisfying. And there are an increasingly large number of quite young and able writers, besides one or two of the alivest among the older ones, who have definitely taken the plunge and gone to the political far Left, and found there that satisfaction in the vision of mankind which is the opposite to the other satisfaction in the vision of God.

This process of going Left is only just beginning in this country. We are only just beginning to get away from the aesthete's doctrine, the art for art's sake which was put across so completely before the war. In America probably most of the writers who count have gone Left, more or less. They find, perhaps, fewer half-way houses than we, with our national genius for compromise, manage to do. And in most other countries writers have realised that they can't stand apart from the life of their times. It seems possible for certain kinds of technicians—doctors, some very skilled and specialised engineers and scientists, and possibly musicians—to stand out of politics, though even they find it hard enough. But we writers have no chance.

We are in touch with life on all sides; part of our job is being sensitive to it. A good many of us combine journalism or publicity of some sort with our other writing, even if our normal job is purely imaginative narrative, conversation and description. In some States we are made to feel officially in touch with the trend and currents of living; I take it that this must be so in Italy. Certainly in Russia. In these countries perhaps writers need not be angry with their work; they may find it thoroughly satisfying. From outside, it is rather hard to tell. It looks as though German and Scandinavian writers were a good deal worried and pulled about. France is still perhaps the most experimental country; one wouldn't be surprised to find a French writer experimenting—and experimenting well—with technique on the top of a barricade which some of his fellow-countrymen had erected across some boulevard. Paris is probably still the city where more people take curious drugs just to see what effects they will have, and where more sexual experiments (as opposed to the ordinary text-book perversion which is provided for in other main cities of the world) are carried on than anywhere else. As for the Great Open Spaces of the world, it is rather hard to tell. The difficulty which I wrote about earlier seems to apply; they are not yet focused. This seems, as far as one can tell from here, to apply also to the very overcrowded parts of the world, like India or China. But considering how little truth we hear about them, I should be sorry to generalise about either country.

Here, then, is a kind of statement of the muddle and distress which we are in, of our lives reflected in our books. To some people it is not a muddle; it is a plain and simple economic consequence. Yet I cannot help feeling that this is over-simplifying, taking too much the eagle's eye view. If one is well in the middle of it, the thing can't but seem a muddle and an angry muddle, and yet at the same time a hopeful and glorious muddle out of which something is yet going to be made. But not, so far as we can see, by us. All that we can do is to state and re-state what is happening, from as many different points of view as possible, and as forcibly as we can. There are plenty of us with force and anger. And, having re-stated and pulled to pieces the muddle, and shown up over and over again—as we shall have to—all the hiding-places, all the artificial peace pools which the runaways think they have attained, we shall end by clearing the ground. We shall have been considerably pricked but there will be a lot less brambles. And then, when we have cleaned things up a bit, we must retire gracefully and, let us hope, with some little pride and honour and happiness, and give over the cleared ground to the new minds. We do not yet know who they will be. Probably we shall dislike them, certainly we shall do so at first. We don't know where they will come from. But we can say that it is on the whole improbable that they will come from the same environment as ourselves, though not impossible. However, we have been able to watch the historical process of inspiration wandering from class to class, and it seems unlikely that it will stay much longer with the professional classes. Yet with any luck our sons and daughters may not be members of the "professional classes" in twenty years. That sort of thing may be over. And chromosomes may meet in new ways.

In the meantime, all I can do now, in spite of anger and worrying, is to go and write another book. It is partly that by now this is the only thing I am good at (and when I say "I", it isn't just this particular little me sitting in front of this particular typewriter that I mean, but a host of similar "I's", for whom I believe I am speaking) and that there is a definite economic incentive to do it. And it is partly that I want to. That I've got to. I've got to do it biologically, just as my children have to play, or just as I have to bear a child at the end of nine months' pregnancy. And it is this wanting to which may perhaps be the best excuse, the most valid answer to anger.

THE VISIONARY GLEAM

SPIRIT OF DEATH   TANGYE LEAN
THE TRIUMPH OF TIME   JAMES LAVER
SABLE GODDESS   DEREK HUDSON
GUBBINS ON LOVE   MICHAEL ROBERTS

SPIRIT OF DEATH

I

IT is night-time in the city.

A vague dome of light hovers over its centre, high and yellow in the middle where the reflections shift up from the most brilliant lights below, and drooping and dull orange at the outskirts where the processions of cars are converging.

The drizzle has faded and gone, leaving the surface of the street wet beneath the slurred swish of the tyres which sweep along into the darkness. The headlights wink and glare, zigzag, then die, and a red spot chases on after the shape that has fled swiftly past. Sometimes a great van drawn by horses comes rumbling and clattering close to the pavement, while the cars swoop out in a wide curve as they flash by and on towards the centre. A few indistinct figures move on the pavements in front of the residential houses, and occasionally one stops, hesitating, on the kerb. In a long, uneven procession, the cars come swishing louder and harder on the wet surface of the road, flashing into life opposite him, then turning and dying to a shadowed whisper as they flee on, blackening into the night.

Into the heart of the orange dome pierce the high white buildings of the city, and from their roofs the lines of cars look like strangely coloured insects all threading in together, as though the great monument in the city square were a decaying carcass with a thousand blackly congested dots crawling slowly round it.

From the roofs lifts shoot down their slender shafts, while floor after floor flashes past their trellised gates of steel. The trellises clang back at the bottom, and on to the marble paving stream the passengers. Threading in and out among one another, they surge into the street and mingle with the hurrying crowds, like a wave unfurling on the shingle, then diving and becoming part of it. Immense red motor-buses thunder past, their sides blotched with shouting advertisements. They lurch onwards with a deep-throated roar which makes an everlasting background to the growls of the hooters, the incessant tinkling of the bicycle bells, and the low purr of the limousines.

Streaks of living light wander in and out among the puddles on the surface of the road, till suddenly they are blotted out by one of the dark masses flying round about them. Then they gleam damply out again, and twitch automatically in time with the street signs from which they were born.

The passers-by are outlined sharp and black against the brightly lit shop windows. The colours change—blood-red and orange and vivid green—but the figures in front of them are black, like the dead patches on the surface of the road. They swarm to and fro, the black figures, identical hundreds of them, leaving here and there a few solitary shapes staring, their heads slightly bent, into the dazzling array of objects in the window. Only where a cinema reaches out a roof of brilliant lights over the pavement are a few colours splashed among the passers-by. Or sometimes the mouth of a theatre sweeps a blazing shaft of whiteness across the road, lighting the silver cloaks of the women in long quivers which shift like liquid, stabbing a brilliant glitter into their jewels, and picking out the starched whiteness of the men's evening dress from the black. The colours glimmer and dart in a seething mass among the audience which is assembling from the street, and sometimes more tawdry gashes show up on the painted mask of a prostitute.

Once the unkempt figure of a tramp treads for a second into the shaft of whiteness, like a moth caught in the rays of a lamp, then he pulls his coat higher around his neck and mooches away into the crowd that shrinks from him.

When the audience comes out it is dazed and stupid, as if bloated with overeating. Some wear the expression stamped on weary faces of business-men as they stream out of their offices to go home and sleep in preparation for another day. The silver cloaks of the women and the sleek blackness of the men fumble together into the waiting cars, which slide off through the streets and mingle again with the roar and the flashing lights and the rushing of the traffic.

ROI SOLEIL—the letters stand out red in thinly brilliant bars, and already the steady, penetrating lilt of jazz throbs into the recesses of the car as the attendant holds the door, and the occupants, their faces still stupid, go in, some of them laughing with laughter which holds in it some of the traffic's noisy artificiality.

The carpets are soft and dead beneath their feet, and give way to the eager, gripping pulse of the dance band. Gradually the laughter stops. Faces set into hard lines. On the surface of the pure white table-cloth fingers drum regularly, regularly drum, like the feet softly thudding on the carpet underneath, softly, regularly thudding, like warm hands plucking mournfully at the strings of a banjo in a far-off tropical sugar plantation. In minute strings the bubbles prick upwards through the glasses of champagne, which are raised swiftly and bumped down again, and the fingers drum on the side of the glass, thudding regularly and automatically, like the twitching lights outside high above the streets, and the reflections that go quivering in and out among the puddles, lighting them and leaving them dead, lighting them and leaving them dead.

Then the dancing.

The bodies are dull and firm. They cling to each other and sway forward and backward, like the fingers tapping on the champagne glass, forward and backward, like the lights twitching into the blackness and out. A score of couples tread jerking to the throb and flutter and cough of the dance band. Some of them are drunk and try thinking they are happy, but their faces are set, strained, expressionless. The pairs of feet shuffle together over the polished boards, shuffle and slide regularly, like the bodies which cling to each other above them, and the fingers tapping on the champagne glass, and the lights quivering and twitching to and fro among the dead puddles outside on the streets of the city.

And meanwhile, away out from the centre square where a few limousines still sweep round the great statue, away from the high white-walled buildings and the dropping lifts, from the long approaching roads with the slur of spinning tyres and clatter of horse-drawn carts, away out beyond where the dome of light droops in dirty orange curtains, there stand the rows of houses. They are low-roofed and squat. A whole family sleeps in one room—father with daughter, and mother with son. The windows are small and there is no clear space on the floor, so that the rooms seem like attics. The streets outside are narrow and black with gutters clogged here and there with refuse. And lining them there are the houses, one after another, squalid, dirty, identical.

In long black rows, stretching away into the unlit dark, they surround the noise and the dazzling whiteness of the centre throughout the night. No sound comes from them, and their very noiselessness seems to intensify the sullen threat which hangs in the blackened, soul-killing air.

So the outskirts of the city and the centre seem to belong to different worlds. But in reality they are one and the same, for they are both part of the noisy superficial struggling of mankind. Noise and movement, that is the keynote of city-life. Like the Sirens' song, it calls to all those who come within its hearing, and anyone who listens and obeys its call is enslaved, and the voice of their independent spirit drowned in the hubbub and rush of physical activity.

In the cities of the world, the physical, mental, and non-spiritual sides of man's activity are developed to their utmost. For the city is dynamic. There everything is telling him to pursue. Sometimes it is mere subsistence that he is pursuing, sometimes society, sometimes money, sometimes pleasure, sometimes women, but always he is pursuing, and the emphasis is laid on the pursuit. It is part of the crunching roar

of the traffic, it twists up with the swollen cylinders of smoke
from the factory chimneys into the sky, it echoes out into the
streets in the shrill voices of the newsvendors, it is in the air
which penetrates to the farthest rooms hidden away from the
centre point of the din. Religion has tried to set up great
barriers against it, cathedrals in the centre of the town, where
the atmosphere is purified and free, and the spirit of man can
escape. But religion cannot live in the city. The power of the
city has killed it. The city sets something pulsing, whether
they know it or not, in the blood of the most unresponsive of
men, so that they, too, are spurred on to join in and become
part of the struggle. And just as in a football crowd the individual does not exist, so the ideas that come to be born of
the city are stereotyped, and the mind has to make a conscious effort if it is to run in any channels other than the
normal ones where the power of the city directs it.

For the voice of the city is not vague or equivocal. It tells
the individual either to enjoy himself feverishly or to employ
himself feverishly. What he does matters little, but it must be
done feverishly and with sufficient noise to drown all other
thoughts.

One thing the city will not tolerate: passivity. And yet
there is one figure who lurks about the corners and stares into
the openings of theatres, a figure who is its very symbol.

It is the tramp.

It is because he is passive that the tramp is so complete an
outcast in the city. It is not his poverty which brands him as
an alien, for in the city poverty is far commoner than wealth.
Nor is it his unkempt raggedness which singles him out as,
slowly and limply, he mooches through the assembling theatre
audience in his purposeless fashion. In him there is something
absolutely unique. All the other passers-by on the pavement
are moving as fast as they can in one direction or the other,
intent, eager, hurried. But he, the tramp, just drifts, and if
he has any business it is an occult and mysterious concern of
his own.

It is to the country and the earth that the tramp belongs, and in the atmosphere of the city he is as out of place as an ageing woman who has borne her children and kept her husband, and, now that she has finished her work, wants only to live with the earth and the trees and slow-moving animals of the country.

Such people hate the city. They hate and fear the hard animosity of it. And the city, in its turn, has no sympathy to waste on them; it has no patience to spare, no time to lose. The city has to hurry on.

The spirit of the city is something that few of the dwellers in it can escape. It takes possession of their bodies and souls and only allows the presence of thoughts and tempers which are in harmony with it. It has a momentum which lasts after its immediate presence has gone, so that a city-dweller who goes into the country takes with him for a while the same city-disposition. Like the throbbing, sensual beat of jazz it eats into one and forces one along with it in the rush of activity. It twitches the mind into the automatic action that it demands, and like jazz it leaves the spirit to care for itself as best it can in the rowdy tumult. And yet, just as there are some people who do not feel the pulsing throb of jazz catching, drug-like, at the strings of their being, so there are some city-dwellers who manage to raise an oasis around themselves, where the rush of practical activity is not allowed to penetrate, and where the imagination and the spirit can roam about unhampered by the roar of noisier life outside. But such people are few—some hundreds of metaphysicians and clergymen, scientists, artists, and writers—and, just like the slouching tramp and the woman who has lived her life, they clash with the spirit of the city, and are misunderstood, disliked, and sometimes even suspected, by the most typical of the mass of inhabitants whose enslavement to the city is complete.

Such is the spirit and atmosphere of the city, an atmosphere opposed to contemplation unless it is practical, and to creation unless it is material.

II

In the suburb it is early morning.

The station crouches high on the bridge in the main street, its outline smudged against the impenetrable greyness of the sky beyond. The street is narrow, like a ruler, and is divided into strips by two pairs of tramlines which cut straight and sharp along its length. The Corporation carts have already cleared the gutters, and the effect is one of neatness, but a strained neatness, as if those who had brought it about had something much uglier to conceal. The shops have only just been opened for the day. Some of the proprietors themselves are cleaning the windows with chamois leather mops, and the cheap display of goods is distorted by the water swilled out on the glass.

From the distance there comes the ugly clanging of a tram's bell, and a large, dirty yellow shape comes clanking over the rails with a metallic grind towards the station. It stops outside, the long conducting arm quivering the wires overhead into a shivering metallic whistle. From inside there come the business-men and the workers and the typists. They are dressed in drab colours, barely distinguishable from the dirty brick of the station walls, and most of them carry cheap cardboard attaché cases.

As they come down the steps of the tram, they roll up their tickets and slip them into the box provided on the side of the car.

Grey and huddled together, with a white rolled paper sticking out from under their arms, they dive down into the suburban station, like so many scared rabbits scurrying into their burrows. Electric trains—smokeless and emasculated— swallow them up and jerk off towards the city.

Then a torpor settles on the suburb.

Beyond the main street, rows of residential houses stretch out, with carefully trimmed privet hedges marking off their gardens from the road. They vary a little in colour, the privet hedges. Some are almost yellow and others are dull green. But that is all the variety of colour that is to be found in the suburb, and everything else is vague and smudged like the colours of the clothes and the outline of the station against the grey back-cloth of the sky.

Gradually the housewives come out into the streets, wearing raincoats and carrying baskets under their arms for the food beyond the fogged windows of the shops. Here and there a milk cart is trundled, belated, down between the privet hedges, and the voice of the milkman penetrates harshly, like the croak of some strange bird, into the dead air of the suburb. Then, one by one, the housewives come back from the main street and, pausing here and there to gossip with a neighbour, return to their houses to see to the housework and doze through the afternoon.

There are no men in the suburb in the daytime. A few assistants and shopkeepers bustle flurriedly about behind the counters in the main street, but they are little people with greasy hair and pinched faces—eunuchs. They have watched the ways and listened to the talk of housekeeping women until they have become like them and seem to fit in with the station and the tramlines and the discreet privet hedges shutting off the front gardens from the road.

Not until it is dark once more do the men come back into the street. Then they come furtively, as though they had waited for the night to cover their retreat from the city; and they sneak back through the streets in the shelter of the fences and the privet hedges, their heads slightly bent, their fingers firmly clutching their attaché cases.

Only when all the lights are out and the man is in bed with his wife does any life come into the suburb. And then it is only half-life—repressed, almost ashamed—between the business-man and his housekeeper lying half-naked beside him.

For the suburb is a place where life does not properly exist, and is replaced by a sort of half-life, an everlasting twilight where there is never either night or morning.

The suburb is a bastard, a strange growth that has come with civilisation. It is a bastard because it is half town, half country, yet neither the one nor the other. No echo of the pulsing throb of the great city is to be found in that main street down which the trams clang their way to the station. Nor is there any of the deep, earthy restfulness of the country clinging to the flower-beds of the gardens. Instead there is an atmosphere of weak artificiality, not unlike that which must permeate a restored building, no matter how carefully it has been restored. The first essential to any atmosphere is that it should have unity—whether unity of dirtiness or unity of cleanliness, unity of age or unity of youth. And the suburb has no unity. It is a bastard, a no-man's land stretching mournfully between the city and the country, partaking of the life of neither.

There is no spirit of energy about the suburb. The men who sleep there at night and who get up there in the morning do not work there in the day. The trains jerk them off in unprotesting batches to the city, and the suburb is left like a body from which the life-blood has been sapped, limp and colourless, with no force of its own. In the daytime it is the land of the housewife, the housekeeper of the business-man, whose soul is gradually ground down and dulled by the interminable round of petty routine, the woman who has lost half her womanhood, who can never know the full thrill of pregnancy.

And so such qualities as the suburb possesses are negative qualities. It is a place built to help in the business of existence, not of life. It is a place where creative work is out of its element. The privet hedges and the tramlines and the shops and their eunuch shopkeepers all frown on great creative endeavour, material, mental, or spiritual. Such things are out of place in the suburb. They seem monstrous and foreign among the petty affairs of the residential houses. It is a place where workers eat and sleep but do not work. It is a shell in which a body never lived.

III

The long, slow slant of the sunlight shows that it is afternoon in the country.

The straw in the great doorway of the barn is shadowed over and lies in scattered heaps which fade into the shadows clustered in the far corners. But the sweet thick scent of the straw has been stirred into life by the sun earlier in the day, and drifts out now over the sun-bleached wisps on the caked earth in front of the barn, curling in and out among the dusty grasses on the roadside, then upwards and out over the white hotness of the road to the creepers which clamber over the farmhouse.

The creepers are part of the farmhouse; they grew up with it out of the earth, shaped it and softened it, so that it has come to share in the richness and the strength of the earth round about its walls. Its windows have grown small and shapeless from the leaves that coil around them, like a heavy frame round a picture which time has darkened into blackness.

It is still and cool and dark inside the windows, and the view outside stands out as though lit by the orange glow of some supernatural arc-lamp.

The curve of a wooded hill rises opposite the farmhouse, and the smoothly swollen outline of a coppice straggled round its summit in a dull blue arc which the sun has distorted by a wash of shadow dropped down the hill from the fringes of the wood, masking half the slope of a meadow and laying its veil across the fallow richness of a ploughed field. The shadow of the wood seems to divide the hill-slope into two, one side dank and fertile, as though pregnant with the richness of freshly fallen rain, and the other bright and alive with all the hidden colours of the sun's rays. Full in the brilliance beside the fallow field there stretches the goldish sweep of a cornfield, ripe, but as yet unbleached like the fairer wisps of straw lying in the sunlight outside the doorway of the old barn. Now and then a faint breath of wind seems to play with the myriad ears, and a shivered wave goes flickering, quivering, among the beads of corn. Almost you can hear the sighing whisper as the metal stems, smelted by the sun, brush swiftly with the stirred air. Here and there the dull red cups of poppies show among the corn, like a mass of blood-glowing cinders from a winter furnace burning with some intense non-human passion.

Away up nearer the coppice, where the shadow of the wood drops down across the meadow, a figure stands, half hidden by the glare of the near-by sunlight. Quite still, he stands there, one hand dangling loose, the other clasping the knob of a massive stick. You would almost say he was gazing at the view, were it not for his unfocused eyes staring dazedly before him. Without moving he stands there leaning on his stick as the blue shade creeps lower down into the valley, and the gold of the cornfield turns to dull orange in the fading light.

From the valley at the bottom of the hill a road twists up towards the farmhouse. Its whiteness is softened by the evening, and as it curves on towards the village beyond the barn it seems to send no sound back from the footsteps of the passers-by, as if the gathering darkness were a carpet thrown across its stones.

The cottages are small and built of dull red brick, with their thatched roofs stretching in among the branches of the trees and disappearing among the shadows of the twilight. The cottages, too, seem part of the earth, and the unkempt flowers rambling aimlessly about them mask the bottom of their walls, the scars where they leave the ground.

An old woman is slowly working the handle of the village pump, and the water glides out limpid and unprotesting into the half-filled pail. The muffled clatter and thump of the handle thuds out gently into the evening air and makes the silence so intense that you can almost feel it. And somehow the thick quietness of the evening, which is caught among the apple-trees and clings to the fading surface of the road and the clambering creepers of the farmhouse, seems connected with the silent figure who still stands like some lifeless scarecrow in

the darkness of the wooded hill. His outline is almost lost, and
it might well be the bent trunk of another tree standing a little
way apart from the huddled dimness of the coppice.

But now the figure moves. As though he were the very
spirit of the place, he comes out with slow, earth-conscious
strides from the shadow of the trees, and for a moment, before
the sun has slid behind the hill, its rays hold him there for a
moment in a blurred confusion of glowing orange, like the
richness of a cathedral window.

It is the tramp.

For the tramp is part of the country. His slow movement
and his laziness seem to have been drawn out of the dank soil
itself, and his silent, aimless plodding is a part of the white
road twisting up the hill and the rich scent of the straw which
drifts about the hill-slope. Among the glaring lights of the
city, with its roar of traffic and pulse of machinery and throb
of jazz, he is an exile, and stares with lost, unseeing eyes at the
lights twitching out and back between the puddles.

In the country the one great universal presence is the
power of the earth. The earth is mother of everything and
master of everything. The shivering metal corn and the heavy-
headed poppies, the grasses by the roadside and the blue
shadow of the coppice, have all grown up out of its silent
fertility. And even the works of man—the farmhouse and the
cottages and the pump—bend eventually to its mastery, and
seem to have grown up with the plants from the earth. The
issue is certain, but it takes time, sometimes years, sometimes
centuries, for the earth to establish its sway. For just as the
spirit of the city is dynamic and its rhythm a neurotic twitch,
so the spirit of the earth and the country is static and its
rhythm deep and slow and earthy like the dankness of a
ploughed field in the springtime.

The stasis of the country is like a heavy scent, like the sweet
smell that goes out from the straw and permeates the whole
hill-slope even to the air playing with the creepers of the farmhouse. It lies like a guiding spirit on the souls of its inhabi-

tants and moves them into harmony with its own quiet slowness. And any echo of the city's rowdy activity clashes like a scream in a cathedral whose air is alive with the murmur of an organ. Occasionally a cheering charabanc careers along the hillside road. The country is quite quiet. It does not protest. It lies there round about, vast, silent, brooding. Yet the threat of its silence is greater than the threat of the squat rows of houses that lie waiting round the centre of the city through the night.

The country is the land of the people who sit and feel. Even the physical effort by which the people rear their substance is slow and as much in harmony with the country as the cornfields and the woods. There is no mental activity to be found in the cottages, or the farms, or even the vicarages. The earth is an enemy of thought. Thought is a foreign weapon that man has forged without her aid, in spite of her. It is the symbol of his separateness, and the germ which originally gave birth to the great city. In proportion as the earth's creatures possess it, so they stand separate from her and partake of another source of life; and in proportion as man is ruled by thought, so he stands separate from her. The quick-thinking businessman and his bustling secretary are as much out of place here as was the tramp in the city. It is only the instinct-guided men, the tramp and the farm-labourer, the farmer and the women who have borne their children, who live at peace in the country.

The country lies like a weight on the mind which is trying to think, trying to create. Quick thoughts are turned to slow thoughts, and slow thoughts gradually to languid, slow sensations. It is not the same as it was in the fever and rush of the city. There is no voice always calling the mind away from itself. The country's ways are not the ways of the city. Here it is as though man had smelt some sweet pervading scent, a scent which holds no distractions in it as the rhythm of the city did, no imperative calls to some other activity, but which drifts in and round about his thoughts, pervades them, clings to them, and gradually, imperceptibly, slows them down and chains them. Then nothing new comes from him. He stands there idle like the tramp in the blue shadow of the hill-slope. He feels the rain sheeting down in the winter, the showers of April flickering across the sunlight, summer blue and breathless overhead, and the homing birds sprayed across the skies in the autumn. All these things he knows in the furthest fibres of his being, but nothing of all that enters into him ever comes from him again. He is like a spellbound audience after a symphony that has ended. The symphony has gone for ever, but it has not vanished: it has gone into the listeners and become part of them, deep and silent, but living still.

So the country, like the town and the suburb, is no birthplace of spiritual creation. All is dumb and slow and old, and newness only comes with the slow growth of plants and animals and birds. And then the newness is only repetition.

For the spirit of the earth is static, like the blue shadow of the wood-crowned hill, and the coiling of the silent road, and the dim figure of the tramp standing there in the half-light on the hill.

IV

All three of them—the city, the country, and even the emasculated suburb—have an atmosphere and a tension of their own. And because they have, all three of them, in their different ways, are obstacles to pure creation, great or little. For in the act of creation the mind is held suspended, with all the ties and connections of the outside world kicked suddenly away. So that life in any of these three places is a shackle to the artist, and life itself—to complete the paradox—is the obstacle, as well as the condition, of creation.

Only in proportion as the influence of an atmosphere is weak on the human mind is it relatively good for the artist. Thus if the throb of the city sets his blood pulsing scarcely at all, while he loves the slow dank fertility of the earth away out in the country, he should stay in the city and not run the risk of being seduced into the stasis of the earth. Or if he is faintly bored in the stillness of the country, and longs to be back in the hurrying throbbing struggle of the city, he should stay out in exile with the earth, where the spirit of the place pulls more weakly.

But in some degree one of the three atmospheres can never be escaped. What the law of gravity is to the scientific world, they are to the spiritual. They hold the spirit back from freedom and chain it to their finite selves.

Newton's apple had to grow wings or it fell. And the creative spirit must grow wings or it, too, falls. One of the three atmospheres will drag it down and fold it in its arms—in the mud where the lights twitch the dead puddles into a gleaming wet brilliance; or in the shelter of the privet hedges where suburban business-men sneak home at night; or in the stillness of the farmhouse which looks out on an orange-lit hill.

THE TRIUMPH OF TIME

THE colours are still so brilliant after the lapse of centuries
and the figures so crowded and heaped upon one another in
their arbitrary perspective, their gowns so elaborately pat-
terned, the helmets of the men so fantastically shaped, their
chains and wands and swords so stiff with gold, that it is a
little difficult at first to tell what is happening. Here and
there, a curled label stands out from the rich background, and
the name on the label is in characters almost Gothic, hard to
decipher and strangely abbreviated like the words in illumin-
ated manuscripts. "Venus" leaps suddenly to the eye, and
"Atropos"; the bearded knight in golden armour is Julius
Caesar; the naked figure of Cupid is three times repeated, the
third time bound. Four unicorns toss their single horn to
heaven; buffaloes have rings of gold through their nostrils,
the elephants are curiously small and their legs have no joints.
The wheels of the gilded cars pass, like so many Juggernauts,
over the portable bodies of human beings—no Hindus these,
but kings, and popes and ladies, huddled in heaps, their rich
gowns crumpled. There is fighting: swords being brandished,
long lances thrust into the sides of enemies, men and women
falling headlong from their pedestals; yet above all the tumult
an unmistakable air of triumph.

It is indeed a Triumph, or rather a series of Triumphs, the
word being understood in the sense in which the Romans used
it when they granted to a general returning victorious his
pageant of spoils and captives through the streets of Rome, he
himself seated on a car or chariot, his head encircled with
laurel. The dominant creed of the Middle Ages frowned upon
such manifestations of human pride. Christian humility was
expected even of kings, and the world saw nothing strange in
the spectacle of a monarch washing the feet of poor men or of

an emperor kneeling in the snow before the Vicar of Christ to
beg his forgiveness. But with the rebirth of Paganism all this
was changed. Glory came down to earth, a glittering bauble
that a man might grasp by reaching out his hand. Poets began to dream of an earthly immortality, and the monarchs of
Christendom became so completely obsessed by the idea of
the Roman triumph that they could not sleep in their beds
nor stay quiet in their kingdoms. This it was that led the
deformed Charles VIII over the Alps to that least lasting of
conquests; this that could draw François I even from the arms
of his mistresses. For this the second Tudor squandered the
money hoarded by the first, and for this the Emperor himself
spent the last years of his brilliant, erratic life elaborating,
with the help of the best artists of his epoch, "The Triumph
of Maximilian"—a triumph which never really took place, in
celebration of a series of victories which had never actually
happened.

Maximilian was not the only monarch to bring out a com-
memorative volume or illustrated souvenir of triumphal processions. The fashion was universal, and even came to be a
recognised part of policy, a means of royal propaganda, the
faint echoes of which can still be heard, even in these days,
when a king opens Parliament. But such ceremonies are mere
relics, out of tune with the times, for although a king may
still be the nominal head of the nation, he no longer *is* the
nation. When Louis XIV cried: *L'État, c'est Moi*, he said no
less than the truth. I suppose it was Prince Albert, with that
unjoyous grasp of realities so characteristic of his temperament, who first, among the princes of the earth, perceived
that times had changed, and that national propaganda for
the future must take the form not of a royal progress but of a
Great Exhibition. The growing glory of the market eclipsed
the fading splendour of the Court.

The triumphal *Entrées* of the Renaissance are an absorbing
study for everyone to whom history is as much the history of
ideas as of events, to all who are interested in reconstructing

the mental backgrounds of past ages, for without such reconstruction past ages must remain incomprehensible. They are also of great importance for the student of the theatre, carrying over as they do the allegorical elements of the morality play into the Court festival, from which developed the Court theatre, from which arose in turn opera and the *pièce à machines*. But I must not be tempted down a by-path in which the surest scholars have lost their way.

The vast literature of triumphal *Entrées* in Italy and France grew steadily during the sixteenth and seventeenth centuries until, at the end of the latter, the Jesuit Menestrier, in his *Traité des Tournois, Joustes, Carousels, et Autres Spectacles Publics*, attempted to deduce from innumerable precedents the exact principles on which such ceremonies should be conducted.

Modern scholars, such as M. Joseph Chartrou in his *Les Entrées Solennelles et Triomphes à la Renaissance*, have approached the subject in a more scientific spirit, and traced the gradual emergence, from the purely feudal elements of the tournament and homage to a monarch, of the more pagan conception of the Triumph. We may note especially, in the *Entrée* which Henri II made into the town of Rouen, a Car of Fame drawn by four winged horses, on the front of which was portrayed Death as a skeleton, bound and vanquished.

Even apart from works issued to enhance the glory of a monarchy, the literature of the Renaissance is full of Triumphs, and the painting too. One may mention in particular the most beautiful illustrated book produced during the Renaissance period, the *Hypnerotomachia Poliphili*, published by Aldo at Venice in 1499. This extraordinary production, better known under the Italian title of *Il Sogno di Polifilo*, the Dream of Poliphilus, has puzzled the wits of the learned ever since its first appearance. Some have seen in it an historical work, some a simple romance of amorous adventure, some an attack on Christian doctrine, some a religious allegory or system of moral philosophy. Some have lent it a cabalistic meaning or have interpreted its voluptuous images in terms of *misteri*

goliardici, blasonici e massonici. But whatever its ultimate
meaning, its importance for us is that it describes a Triumph
of Love which had a profound influence on the imagination
of contemporaries.

In painting, the wealth of Triumphs is astonishing, not only
in Italy and France but in Germany and Flanders. There
are Triumphs by Georg Pencz, by Jost Amman, by Peter
Breughel, by Martin Heemskerk. Holbein painted a Triumph
of Riches and a Triumph of Poverty for the merchants of
London; Hans Sebald Beham devised a Triumph of Women.
There are Triumphs of Religion, of Fortune, of Prudery, of
Impiety; there are Triumphs of Beggary, Triumphs of Pol-
troonery, Triumphs of Flora.

In Italy Triumphs were painted by Francesco Mantegna,
Bernardino Campi, Bonifacio di Verona, and in the smaller
world of line engraving and book-illustration Triumphs are
innumerable. The tapestry weavers of Arras and neighbouring
towns were particularly fond of Triumphs, and examples of
their work are to be found in Madrid, Vienna, Berlin, Hampton Court and South Kensington. It was the tapestries at the
two latter places that I was describing in the opening paragraphs of this essay.

The curious thing is that as these various Triumphs are
traced backward in Time they grow more and more similar
to one another, so similar that it is obvious that the theme and
its imagery must be derived from a common source. There is
a set in the Uffizi executed by Matteo de' Pasti in 1441, and
these bear the closest resemblance in subject-matter, although
not in actual handling, to the series attributed to Andrea
Vanni painted before 1414 and now in the Accademia at
Siena. The earlier we go the less ravelled becomes the thread.
Details differ but the form of the pageant is always the same,
the underlying idea constant. Whence comes this idea, potent
enough to stir the imaginations of so many artists, fruitful
enough to draw from them such rich fruits of their own
invention?

All these Triumphs can be traced back to one book, printed first at Venice in 1470, but existing in manuscript for more than a hundred years previously: *I Trionfi* of Petrarch. Few men have had so much influence on human sentiment, at least in western Europe, and much of the peculiar form and colour of the Renaissance must remain incomprehensible to us unless we know something of the life of the poet and how he came to write *The Triumphs*.

Francesco Petrarca, Francis Petrarch, was born at Arezzo in 1304. His father was the friend of Dante, and like Dante was a Ghibelline banished from Florence. The fact is of importance because it helps to place Petrarch so exactly in his period, and marks also the gulf that yawns between him and his great predecessor; for if Dante was the last of the great mediaevals, Petrarch was the first of the moderns. When he was still a child his father removed his family to Avignon, to which city Clement V had transferred the papal court. The boy was intended for a lawyer and to that end was set to study at the University of Montpellier; but the Canon Law had less attraction for his mind than Virgil and Cicero. He read also the works of the troubadours, and imbibed from them the romantic ideal of love which was to be so manifest in his own writings and which is so conspicuously absent from the writings of the ancient world.

The troubadours have never received full credit—or discredit—for this particular contribution to human sensibility. Even Dante learned from them, and their influence has lasted down to our own day. Indeed it was never stronger or more widespread, and still provides a flourishing industry with its chief stock in trade. I wonder if Greta Garbo and Constance Bennett realise that they are still drawing dividends from investments made in the south of France in the twelfth and thirteenth centuries.

Even Petrarch did not give them full credit. Their influence formed the permanent background of his emotions, but his intellectual life moved on what he considered to be a higher plane. Lost in the study of the ancient writings he began to neglect the Law altogether, and his father, learning of this, descended upon him one day in wrath, burned his classical library, and sent him to the University of Bologna to mend his ways.

However, when Petrarch was twenty his father died, leaving him penniless. He returned to Avignon, where his personal charm, wit and learning soon made him friends and found him patrons in the cultivated society of the papal court. It was at Avignon, when attending mass, on Holy Monday, the 6th April, 1327, at six o'clock in the morning, that he first saw Laura and fell in love with her at first sight. His passion was not returned, for Laura was the wife of Hugues de Sade, and virtuous. Perhaps Petrarch never expected any physical satisfaction, but, like a true troubadour, he fed the flame in his imagination until Laura became for him the object of a cult and the main preoccupation of his writings—not, be it noted, of his serious works, which were in Latin, but of those verses in the vulgar tongue which he hoped might be read by women and children for their entertainment, but on which he hardly expected that any lasting fame could be based.

The idea of fame obsessed him. With the glories of the Romans ever before his eyes he sought to rival them in every department, at least of literature. He would be a poet as great as Virgil, a philosopher as great as Cicero (for Cicero passed for a philosopher), an historian as great as Livy; and it was in an endeavour to emulate these writers that he produced *Africa* and *De Viris illustribus*.

These works were written for the most part in the solitudes of Vaucluse, the closed valley to which he retired in disgust from the worldly vanities of Avignon, and it was to his house at Vaucluse that two messengers came who might have satisfied any man's desire for honour. Dramatic propriety demands that they should have set foot on his doorstep at the same moment. Actually a few hours elapsed between their arrival, but at least they arrived on the same day. One was

from the Chancellor of the University of Paris inviting him to
receive a crown of laurel; the other was from the Roman
senate inviting him to come to Rome in order that he might
be crowned in the Capitol. Petrarch thanked both envoys,
but he accepted the Roman triumph.

As it was Robert of Anjou, King of Naples, who had moved
the Roman senate to invite him, Petrarch went to Naples
first, and was received there with every symbol of honour, the
king taking off his own cloak and casting it round the poet.
In Rome itself his triumph was such as had not been seen
since the fall of the Empire. The old Roman spirit was
stirring again; Petrarch made friends with Rienzi and tried
to induce the Pope to return from Avignon.

It was on 8th April, 1341, that he received his crown, but
the next few years were years of bitter disillusionment. The
Pope preferred to stay in Avignon; the flame lit by Rienzi
proved a fire of straw; the unification of Italy lay more than
six centuries into the future. Worst of all, Laura died in the
plague of 1348, that same plague which Boccaccio describes
so vividly in the beginning of the *Decamerone*.

Petrarch went once more into retirement, partly at Vau-
cluse (his transalpine Parnassus) and partly at a house in
Parma (his cisalpine Parnassus). Thus with one foot in
France and one in Italy he passed the remainder of his days.

Perhaps he set more store by his Italian writings than his
contemporaries supposed; for, although he gave no name,
other than "Fragments in the vulgar tongue", to the book in
which they were collected, he polished and repolished them
until his death, and to the *Sonetti* and the *Canzoni* in which he
had celebrated Laura, he added *The Triumphs*.

In these he sought, as most poets do sooner or later, to distil
the essence of his philosophy into a single poem. Wordsworth
tried to do it in *The Prelude* and *The Excursion*, and Tennyson
in the *Idylls of the King*. Wordsworth only partially succeeded,
and Tennyson, exquisite poet as he was, had perhaps nothing
particularly profound to distil. But in *The Triumphs* we shall

find the whole of Petrarch, a whole as rounded and complete as that of Dante, and perhaps more important for the modern world.

The Triumphs form a series of allegorical visions, similar to those popularised by the Provençal poets, and the metre is that in which the *Divina Comedia* is written. The subjects however are not arbitrarily chosen like those of the troubadours, and the sequence represents a logical development. There are six Triumphs: the Triumph of Love, the Triumph of Chastity, the Triumph of Death, or Fate, the Triumph of Fame, the Triumph of Time, and the Triumph of Divinity. Love triumphs over all men, from the philosopher Aristotle bestridden like an ass by his mistress to the wizard Virgil suspended between earth and heaven in a basket. Chastity triumphs over Love, but Death or Fate triumphs over Chastity. Fame triumphs over Death, and Time triumphs over Fame. Almost half-heartedly, as it seems, Petrarch added the Triumph of Divinity over Time, but from the series of tapestries at South Kensington and at Hampton Court the Triumph of Divinity is missing, so that the series ends with the Triumph of Time.

With the wealth of allegory embroidered by Petrarch upon these conceptions, with the actual texture of his poem, we are not here concerned. Nor is it necessary to linger over all the parts into which the work is divided. Love has its triumphs yet, although that once proud name has been abandoned for the pseudo-scientific one of "sex-appeal". Chastity, perhaps, is not so triumphant as it was, but Death still triumphs over both Love and Chastity. Fame, grown hoarse with shouting during a man's lifetime, may still find breath to whisper over his grave. And Time—the Triumphs of Time are everywhere; they are the very hall-mark of our epoch, the most obvious fact of the modern world, and of that modern world Petrarch is the first great figure. He, more than any other single person, inaugurated the Triumph of Time.

The Middle Ages too had its Triumphs. Giotto's frescoes in the Lower Church at Assisi represent the Triumph of Chastity,

Poverty, Obedience, and St Francis. There is in the Campo
Santo at Pisa a Triumph of Death attributed to Orcagna.
Ambrogio Lorenzetti painted a Triumph of Good Government for the *palazzo pubblica* at Siena. In the Spanish Chapel
of Santa Maria Novella at Florence there is a famous fresco
depicting the Triumph of St Thomas Aquinas, or, more
strictly, the Triumph of Divinity with the Divine Doctor in
the place of honour. On either side of him, and above and
below, sit all the other Christian sages. They do not move, for
they have attained truth, and to move would be to deviate into
error. All these mediaeval triumphs are static. But Petrarch
gave the Triumph wheels, so that what had been a throne became a car; what had been a tableau became a procession.

In this, as in so many of his innovations, Petrarch was
merely reaching back to the ancient world which he admired
so much. The Roman triumph was essentially a movement,
and movement, perpetual expansion, was a necessity for the
Empire. The *Pax Romana* was the beginning of the decline and
fall, for Imperial Rome lived on its conquests, and, when the
limit of expansion was reached, it decayed. Perhaps we are
witnessing something of the same kind in the industrial world
of to-day, which must find new markets or perish.

The Greeks themselves, unless Plato be an exception, had
had no static view of the Universe. Their speculative but un-
devotional minds were unable to resist the conclusion that
Time devours his own children and that everything passes
away. Even Olympus was not exempt from change, for the
very gods had beheld one dynasty give place to another and
were themselves the helpless pawns of destiny. But these
views, common enough in the ancient world, had been obscured by the birth of Christianity and the emergence of a
God unshakably immortal, and inevitably victorious. The
feeling of stability is always obtainable by minds that take
enough for granted.

The men of the Middle Ages had forgotten the philosophy
of flux; they looked for an abiding city, formed partly in their

pious fancy by that vision of the New Jerusalem which the author of the Book of the Revelation of St John the Divine had elaborated with such a wealth of jacinth, sardonyx and chrysoprase, such gates of pearl, such streets of gold, such walls of jasper; partly by the *Civitas Dei* of St Augustine.

> The poet saith: Dear City of Cecrops;
> Shall not I say: Dear City of God?

And partly, for reasons obvious enough, by the idea of Rome, the throne of the Caesars, the chair of Peter, the anointing-place of Charlemagne.

The mediaeval period, also, was an age of lawlessness, in which the open country was unsafe. To the modern, the country is a place to which he flees for peace; to the mediaeval the town, or at least the castle, was a place to which he fled for safety. The city, with its high walls, its massive bastions, its solid gates, was his refuge and his fortress, while above the walls and beyond the bastions he could see the *flèche* of his cathedral, God's castle, which impious feet feared to enter. Even the criminal could find in the sanctuary Sanctuary.

So the man of the Middle Ages, looking from his fields upon the neighbouring town, thought of Rome as merely an enlargement of that image, a city set upon seven hills instead of upon one, and heaven itself as merely a yet grander city, inviolable as the city of Emperor and Pope had not been inviolable, and eternal in a truer sense than Rome. His very conception of the Universe was narrowed to the thought of a place.

It is a commonplace that mediaeval thought found its culmination in the great tripartite poem of Dante, and the glory of that achievement still throws its shadow over the imagination of the world. Dante clothed the dry bones of Aquinas with flesh and blood, and the imagery which he invented is still so much alive that we tend to think of it as having always formed part of Catholic doctrine, just as many Protestants are almost persuaded that the Slough of Despond,

Doubting Castle and the House of the Interpreter form part of the Bible story.

It is unnecessary to stress the static character of Dante's Universe. One might penetrate to the lowest circle of Hell or the highest circle of Heaven, but the circles themselves were fixed and unchangeable, with God and the three-headed monster as their nodal points. In spite of the horrors of the Inferno there was something comforting in such a conception, precisely because it did not stretch the imagination too far, because it offered to the mind a Universe with conceivable boundaries, a Universe too—and this again in spite of Hell's torments—in which Eternal Justice reigned. Modern sensibility is revolted by the frozen lake and the brimstone pit, but to those who could accept it Dante's vision undoubtedly brought comfort, because it endowed the Universe with a purpose and a meaning. It was to be followed, however, by very different notions.

Time was always a stream—such a conception was too obvious to escape—but to the mediaeval mind it was a stream studded with islands, like the Seine at Paris. The main island, as at Paris, was *la cité*, and in its centre rose the Church. To the modern mind Time is also a stream, but there are no islands in it at all. At the most, a raft, like the rafts of logs brought down the Amazon or the Mississippi, keeps afloat by skilful steering and travels with the current. Is it not even a point of pride with us to be abreast of the time? Time does not flow over us; it carries us with it.

The mediaeval felt solid earth beneath his feet. The sun and moon revolved round him, each set firmly in its crystal sphere. They were God's lamps, the sun to lighten the day and the moon to lighten the night, and God at His will might delay either in order to help one of His favourites in battle. The earth was flat, and if one went too far one might fall over the edge.

Then came the voyages of discovery, and the astonishment of the first circumnavigators to find on their return that they

were a day out of their reckoning. Then the theories of
Copernicus and the experiments of Galileo, and the Christian
world saw its cosmogony falling about its ears. Who could tell
what might not be involved in such a fall? The Church was
alarmed, and rightly, and compelled Galileo to retract his
opinions. It was a vain effort, for the earth's reassuring immobility was gone for ever. It became a mere pendulum
swung in the heavens to record the passage of Time.

The full fruits of this new conception of the Universe were
not immediately apparent, indeed they did not become entirely manifest until the end of the eighteenth century. Till
then the notion of Place still overlaid the notion of Time, so
that men thought even of Antiquity rather as a region than as
a period. Rome itself was a kind of lost Atlantis. Something
of the same notion still clings about our conception of China,
so that we must do a violence to our imagination to realise
that the Dynasty of Han was contemporaneous with the Empire of Justinian, and that human beings could travel from
one to the other—and did so, when the two monks brought
the first silkworms to Byzantium, hidden in a hollow cane.

The mind hungers for a comprehensible completeness and
it is natural for men to think of epochs as islands, just as it is
natural for them to think the world the centre of the Universe
surrounded by concentric circles which are the tracks of the
planets and bounded by the Primum Mobile. To accept the
Copernican theory was to fly in the face of every instinct
of the mind. To accept the temporal interpretation of the
world was to exchange a group of concrete images—as solid
as a row of statues—for a perplexing series of dissolving views.
The intelligence detests blurred outlines and ragged edges,
and what we ask of all things from a world to a cherry-stone
is that they should "come clean".

The eighteenth century "comes clean", that is to say, it
exists in our imaginations as an entity with definite boundaries, and although, of course, this entity has no real existence, the fact that it is possible to form it is sufficiently

curious. It almost seems as if the eighteenth century had something of the timelessness of the mediaeval period. It saw the attempt, the last attempt, to erect a religious philosophy on the basis of pure rationality. It saw the invention of a costume which seemed about to stereotype itself for ever— buckled shoes, skirted coat, sword, wig and three-cornered hat. It is worth noting that whereas anyone can tell James I from Charles I at a single glance, only the expert can tell George I from George II. Society seemed, as it seemed in the Middle Ages, to have set solid. There appeared to Dr Johnson and his contemporaries no reason why the world should ever be very different from what it was. But towards the end of the century it became obvious that this static quality was de- lusive. The day outside the orangery windows darkened; the Sèvres tea-cups rattled with the vibration of an approaching storm. *Après nous le déluge!* It became a commonplace that change of a catastrophic kind was fast approaching. The stream of Time flowed onward the more strongly for this temporary check and the men and women of the end of the eighteenth century were more time-conscious than anyone had ever been before. There was a new Renaissance, a new looking to the Past, and with greater knowledge the spectacle of the Past was infinitely extended.

The result was the addition of a new province to human sensibility. The ancient Greek had dreamed of the Golden Age, the man of the Renaissance had looked back with long- ing to an antiquity three parts imagination. The Jewish legend of the Garden of Eden is a proof of how constant, in any age, is such a sentiment. But the beginning of the nineteenth century saw something entirely different, an admiration of the Past not because it was better but simply because it was past. No one (no one that is at the beginning of the nine- teenth century, for an attempt has been made to persuade us within recent years) believed that the mediaeval period was a better age to live in, a more comfortable age, safer for life and limb. The vision of the Past had become so deeply suf-

fused by emotion that merely thinking about it was sufficient
to conjure up a delicious emotion, a nostalgia as for some
vanished youth.

The progress of this sentiment is fairly easy to determine.
The men of the Renaissance admired the ruins in Rome
because they had been Roman temples. The men of the
eighteenth century admired them because they were ruins.
They even erected similar ruins in their own parks, and
shattered Corinthian columns and broken arches appeared
in English landscape. There is in the Victoria and Albert
Museum a drawing by one of the brothers Adam, and on it is
plainly written, "Design for a Ruin". Your Roman or your
Greek would have thought a designer of ruins visited by the
gods with some strange madness. Perhaps he was, but, if
so, his disease was universal. It was not long in spreading
throughout all classes and including in its symptoms not only
a hunger for Roman ruins, but for any ruins. There was even
a reaction against classical remains and a marked preference
for Gothic.

In literature we have *The Castle of Otranto*. Horace Walpole
was one of those excessively sensitive natures which are like
very delicate meteorological instruments recording the approach of an atmospheric disturbance long before the hands
of ordinary barometers have moved from "Set fair". But
Walpole was followed by "Monk" Lewis and a whole tribe,
while head and shoulders above them all stands the tall figure
of Sir Walter Scott. Moonlight shone through the broken
windows of ruined abbeys, knights clashed together in tourney,
ladies in steeple-caps waved white kerchiefs from castle windows, monkerie came back into fashion, ghosts walked again.

These things were far from being merely literary properties, although in England their influence was prevented
from spreading quickly by Protestantism and the Evangelical
reaction. In France there was no such safeguard, and there
the influence of Scott was more than matched by that of
Chateaubriand.

It is true that the Vicomte has fallen now a little out of fashion, but that is only because his work is accomplished, so completely accomplished that the more obvious aspects of that work hardly need discussion. The *philosophe* of the eighteenth century took it for granted that Christianity was a dying creed. Some thought it would die quickly, some that it would die slowly, but all thought that it would die. And then, after that least reasonable of all Feasts of Reason when the worship-hungry people of Paris enthroned a prostitute on the altar of Notre-Dame, the wave of reaction flowed back in full strength, and riding on the crest of the wave like a magnificent galleon of a former age, its bulwarks painted with saints' pictures and its sails bright with the Emblems of the Passion, Chateaubriand's splendid ship rode into harbour. The *Génie du Christianisme* seemed to the men of its epoch like a new revelation, as if Faith itself had been born again.

Christianity had indeed been born again, but with a difference, and it is this difference that I want to consider. For the early Christians their religion was the religion of the future to which the world would one day be compelled to conform; for a man like Bossuet, it was the religion of the present, taking its natural place in the accepted order of temporalities. In the early nineteenth century Christianity became for the first time the religion of the past, or rather (for it had been that to the *philosophes*, who had therefore despised it) the fact that it was the religion of the past became one of its chief attractions; for very many minds and temperaments its only attraction.

This curious change is reflected in the history of church architecture. It had seemed quite natural to Wren to build churches in the style of his own day, just as Pope Julius before him had not hesitated to destroy old St Peter's in order to build the new. Until the early nineteenth century this was the natural attitude, and enough late Georgian churches exist in London to remind us how simply and innocently it was possible to construct a place of worship. But the neo-Gothic builder was not only constructing a place of worship, he was building a stage set, and it is significant that the first reproductions of ecclesiastical Gothic (Strawberry Hill was not ecclesiastical, nor Fonthill, and both were rich men's whims) were actually seen on the stage. William Capon preceded Pugin. Soon, imitation Gothic had become the accepted stage-setting for the Anglican liturgy, and before the century was out it became almost impossible to think of any other. What counter-influence might have been exercised by Wren's churches was nullified by the fact that, with the dwindling of the population of central London, these churches became increasingly deserted. An exception must be made in favour of the Nonconformists, who continued to build in a style which might be described either as debased Georgian or neo-Baptist; but Nonconformists are notoriously deficient in the historical sense.

The point I wish to emphasise is that all this care for appropriateness of *décor*, this reaching back to the emotions of a past age, means something entirely new in men's attitude to worship. Whether they are aware of it or not, their experiences in church have moved one degree further from reality. A sense of period has entered into their devotions, and religion has taken on something of the quality of a "period piece". Chateaubriand himself is a crowning example of this tendency and his great book is at least as much a monument to romanticism as a monument to Christianity. Romanticism is Time grown self-conscious.

This new self-consciousness had, in the arts, results which were almost wholly unfortunate. Particularly was this true of the decorative arts, which for the first time in history became obsessed with the vision of what had gone before them. The men of the Renaissance had gone back to Rome for their inspiration, but the very fragmentary nature of the discoveries on which their work was based prevented them from being mere servile copyists. The new St Peter's is not in the least like any building existing at the time of the Caesars. Its

architects took Roman *motifs* but subdued them to their own
inspiration. But the nineteenth century was fatally learned
and fatally romantic, and its reproduction of Gothic churches
was at best frigid, at worst preposterous, a copy which left
out the essential qualities of the original and substituted for
them nothing of its own.

In the minor arts there was a collapse of craftsmanship due
in part to Industrialism but even more due to the new admiration for former ages. From the situation thus created we
are only just beginning to escape, for we are still under the
tyranny of "period" decoration. A modern decorator asked
to adorn a house almost always asks his employer what
"style" he should use. Shall it be Tudor, or Jacobean, or
rococo, or, in the United States, Spanish-American or "Old
Colonial"? Such questions would have been incomprehensible to the men of former epochs, when Time had not yet
triumphed over beauty, nor turned the houses of the rich into
museums of relics.

In the realm of pure philosophy, although I approach its
border with trepidation, it was, I suppose, Hegel who was
first conscious of the time-perspective and who made it an
integral part of his system. But although Hegel could call the
events of Time the elements and the words of an eternal
language, he was too much of an idealist—too much *the*
idealist—to see all the implications of his own statement.
These implications have been worked out by his remote followers, the neo-idealists, for whom in the words of J. A. Gunn
"the fundamental Dialectic is the Dialectic of History; all
other Dialectics depend on it". Croce, in his *What is living
and what is dead in the philosophy of Hegel,* has insisted on
the modifications which Time has wrought in the Hegelian
system.

Among the scientists the same influences were at work, and
led rapidly to the rise of comparative biology and the formula-
tion of the doctrine of evolution. Perhaps no single idea has
so completely revolutionised every department of human

thought since the earth ceased to be the centre of the Universe.
Darwin was far from being the only worker in this field, but
it was he who gave the doctrine its greatest publicity, and
brought down upon himself the anger of those whose chief
desire in religion was the sensation of security. Petrarch
pictured Time as vanquished by Divinity, but in the nineteenth century it was Divinity that was compelled to stand
on the defensive. Darwin's pet doctrine of automatic natural
selection has been modified or abandoned, but the theory of
evolution has spread from biology to almost every science, and
changed the colour of every idea we possess. It has even in-
vaded theology itself and there are chairs at our universities
for the study of the history of religion. To the mediaeval mind
religion had no history. It was either true or false; if it were
false it was not really religion at all; if it were true it was the
truth once and for all delivered to the saints.

The attitude of mind induced by the doctrine of evolution
made this position untenable. Christianity became merely
one of many religions, and the difference between it and the
others a difference in degree instead of a difference in kind.
It was even seen to be composed of many strands, some common to all religions, some conditioned by its own particular
history. When the learned had deducted from Christianity
the contributions of Greek mystery-religions, of the Stoics,
of Alexandrian neo-Platonists, of Jewish mythology and of
Roman Law, what remained? The sayings of a certain
Essene of Galilee, whose teachings have never exercised a
very prominent influence on Christian practice, or even on
Christian precept. All these elements we have mentioned may
be very good things. I think most of them are. They may
represent fundamental desires of the human spirit. They
certainly do. But to admit this is to admit that religion sinks
to a department of psychology, and ceases to fulfil its chief
function, which is to comfort mankind with the idea of permanence. It is not thus that Divinity triumphs over Time.

The influence of the same spirit was even more apparent in

the work of the nineteenth-century social reformers. One has
only to note the difference between Rousseau and Marx to be
aware of yet another triumph of the *Zeitgeist*. For the former
History was merely a mistake. "Man was born free, and is
now everywhere in chains." Return to Nature, abolish kings
and priests, and there will be no difficulty in re-establishing
the Golden Age. The doctrines of Shelley are not essentially
different, but with Marx we have already entered a new
world. The author of *Das Kapital* is positively obsessed with
History, so much so that he falls headlong into a mechanistic
determinism from which his followers have not yet escaped.
They think of Communism as the inevitable term of a series of
historical forms; but the latest child of Time has no more hope
of immortality than any of the others.

Marx prophesied the inevitable death of Capitalism once
it had given birth to its child, Communism. Other thinkers
were not so pessimistic—or optimistic, if you are a Communist.
They believed in Progress, that is to say, they envisaged a
world in which the ideals of nineteenth-century Liberalism
would gradually come to be more and more completely accepted. Votes for forty-shilling freeholders should be followed
by votes for everybody; more and more heads should be
counted and fewer broken all over the world. The brood of
the Mother of Parliaments should be like the Seed of Jacob,
as the sands of the sea for number.

This idea of Progress, which must always be repugnant to
neo-Platonists like the Dean of St Paul's, is full of absurdities,
and it is not difficult to turn it into ridicule. It is the political
Philosophy of Becoming—the notion that you may advance
steadily without going anywhere in particular, for the Pro-
gressive always hesitates to lay down the lines of his Utopia.
But I am not here concerned with the criticism of Liberalism,
nor is it necessary for us to decide whether Progress be an
illusion or no. It is sufficient to note that the whole doctrine
is deeply tinged with the consciousness of Time, indeed erects
Time into a new deity replacing all others.

9-2

Time inevitably dominates a democratic state. Place is forgotten. For Democracy there are no holy places, only good times coming. In fact, Democracy might be defined as a condition of affairs in which nobody knows his place, but only the time—at which he knocks off. Every construction implies a Place, but Time is the great leveller. Even in the visible aspects of things Time is now victorious, so that there is less difference between (shall we say) New York and Chicago, than between New York in 1900 and New York in 1930. Place is Vishnu, the Preserver; Time is Siva, the Destroyer.

As Time pursues its conquests local loyalties yield to a kind of temporal loyalty, as though one should cease to be a Yorkshireman and become merely a man of the post-war epoch. Even morality is now conditioned by Time and not by Place. No more do women veil their faces in Constantinople and emphasise their hips in Holland. Now they expose their legs in 1927 and their bare backs in 1933. In former days Europeans in Turkey were in danger of molestation for immodesty in dress. It is fortunate for us, or for our women, that we cannot wander at will from one year into another, for if we did they would certainly be arrested for indecent exposure.

Nothing illustrates the Triumph of Time more clearly than the growing dominance of fashion, although like so many Renaissance influences it did not find its full expression until the nineteenth century. In the Middle Ages, when Place was more important than Time, even the cut of clothes was regional rather than temporal. Remain in your own village and everything was the same for generations; travel into the next parish and everything was changed. But ignoring local differences, such differences as are still to be seen between the peasant costume of neighbouring Swiss cantons, or neighbouring Dutch towns, the dress of western Europe remained almost unaltered from the time of Charlemagne to the end of the fourteenth century. The dress of each rank was stereotyped. The knight can always be distinguished from the burgess, but only the expert can tell the difference between the lady of 1100 and the lady of 1200. It needs no expert to distinguish between 1912 and 1930; and this change, although we take it so completely for granted, is really of profound significance and importance. It is nothing less than the difference between two conceptions of the Universe.

The speeding up of fashion's changes is due to several causes, chiefly to large-scale production and the survival of snobbery into a democratic world. The breakdown of the social hierarchy leaves every woman (for man has ceased to compete) free to dress as well as she can afford, with the result that the only possible superiority is the slight one of cut or material, or the short one of adopting a new fashion a little sooner than her neighbours. The latest creations of the great Paris *couturier* are copied and duplicated almost as soon as they appear in the shops, so that the fashionable woman is forced to adopt something still newer in order to preserve her advantage.

It all seems very wasteful and almost meaningless, this discarding of old clothes in order to conform to the whim of half a dozen French designers, but the matter is not quite so simple as that. The designers are not their own masters. They can only introduce an innovation if it happens to be in accordance with the spirit of the age. What this means precisely I do not know, but I am convinced that it means something, for although the fashions of to-day appear almost purely arbitrary, the fashions of a few years ago, as soon as they are far enough removed to be seen in perspective, have always a strange appropriateness, as if the people of the past could have clothed themselves in no other fashion. This may be nothing but a trick of the imagination, but if so it is one of imagination's inevitable tricks.

Nothing is more curious than the utter slavery of contemporaries to the fashion of the moment. I have in my possession two photographs of Mrs Bancroft as Peg Woffington, one taken in 1875 and one in 1880. Now the Bancrofts prided themselves on their historical accuracy, and yet it is quite possible to date the two photographs with absolute certainty. Indeed they hardly appear to us to have any eighteenth-century character at all.

There is in the bishop's palace at Chichester a famous wall-painting of the Virgin and Child, known as the Chichester Roundel, and there are at South Kensington two copies of this, one made recently by Professor Tristram, which seems an absolute replica of the original, and one made in 1840. The latter, while done by an artist who was obviously making every effort to be faithful, has the oddest look of the youthful Queen Victoria.

One is almost driven to believe in the mystical conception of a *Zeitgeist* who determines for us every detail of our lives, down to gestures, turns of phrase, and even thoughts. It is a distasteful notion, and we must resist it if we are to preserve our faith in our own individuality. But I find it easy enough to believe of other people. Ideas are "in the air" and we catch them as we catch influenza. Only the strongest constitutions resist. Only the greatest men transcend the *Zeitgeist*; that is what we mean when we say they are immortal. But most of us are as firmly embedded in Time as flies in amber, or rather as stones in a glacier, ever moving irresistibly onward to some unthinkable moraine below.

How shall we fight against Time? The modern age makes a typical reply with the one word "Speed". But this is a delusion. Every device for quick transport only makes our servitude more apparent, and a century of railways has done much to rivet upon human consciousness the tyranny of Time. The ancients were content to say, "Let us meet at sundown", or "Let us set out at sunrise", or "Let us call a halt at noon". With the invention of clocks, men began to pay obedience to the arbitrary divisions on the faces of clocks, and to think in terms of hours. But only the tyranny of railway time-tables could have forced a procrastinating humanity to think in terms of minutes. The notion that the 10.13 from Euston waits for no man, although not strictly true, is burned into our consciousness, as if it were a law of Nature. Bradshaw was the new Rhadamanthus and from his judgments there was no appeal.

No doubt the invention of motor-car and aeroplane has transferred the emphasis from "time when" to "time during which", but this is only to make matters worse. In reality all breaking of speed records is another victory over Place. To be in London for breakfast and Paris for lunch is to blur still further the distinction between places; it is to intensify the defeat of locality; it is to decrease the size of the world. It is no victory over Time.

The answer of the modern age is to go faster still, and as the question of speed is so closely bound up with recent theories of Time, we must pause over it for a moment longer. If it were possible to fly from London to New York, not in thirty hours, but in three, the airman would arrive at his destination before he set out. It would be no question of breakfasting in London and lunching in New York. He could lunch in London and have breakfast in New York on the same day. There is even an island in the central Pacific through which the Date Line runs. Its inhabitants, if they cared for such an amusement, could spend their whole time walking from Wednesday into Tuesday and back again. But this, although confusing, does not delay for a single instant the flight of Time.

So much may seem obvious, yet some scientists have got themselves into a fearful tangle over what they call the relativity of Time. The earth itself being a somewhat unreliable clock, astronomers are compelled to fall back on sidereal time, time measured by the movements of the stars. The only way in which we can tell the positions of the stars is by the light that reaches us from them; but the speed of light is unfortunately not infinite. It takes eight minutes to reach us even from the sun, and thousands of years from some of the stars. Before the light from a star reaches us, the star itself has moved on.

If we could travel from the earth in a projectile at a speed greater than that of light, and had telescopes strong enough to study the earth as we flew from it, the events of history would be seen to move backwards. Would not this be a victory of speed over Time? Or is it nothing more complicated than a delay (so to speak) in the post? If a bride on her honeymoon sends postcards to her mother from every place she stays in, does it alter the nature of Time if the mother only receives the Paris postcard when her daughter is already in Florence? If on her way home the Paris postcard, posted a day later than the one in Florence, actually arrives before it, does this mean any more than that the daughter is travelling faster than the post? Thus the fact that the imaginary scientist is travelling faster than light proves nothing more than that he is travelling faster than light.

There are indeed only two ways by which the Triumph of Time may be brought to an end: by the Triumph of Divinity, the victory of a religion by believing in which the mortal can put on immortality, or by the annihilation of Space, the cessation of the world of events, for events are the very stuff of Time, and when they cease Time ceases too.

I am, of course, aware that in these remarks I have not even attempted to debate the profound philosophical problems involved. Of the nature of Time I have preferred to say nothing because I know nothing and lack the metaphysical equipment to make nothing sound like a great deal. The difficulties in which even men of science have found themselves involved since they abandoned the Newtonian doctrine of Absolute Time I have rather mentioned than ventured to discuss.

With Einstein's theory of relativity, with Maritain's description of it as true physics but pseudo-metaphysics, with Bergson's two fictitious characters of Peter and Paul, dwelling in two different systems in relative motion to each other, with Nordmann's proposal to change their names to Thomas and Louis, and with J. A. Gunn's final emendation to Thomas and George, with the "relativity of simultaneity", with Bergsonian *durée* or psychological time, with time that dilates and contracts, with light that bends, with illusory futures and projected presents, with the *Zeitpunkt* and the *Weltraum*, with the *Raumpunkt* and the *Zeitström*, with the Lorentz-Fitzgerald equations and the Michelson-Morley experiment the present essay is not concerned.

As a good Humanist I have striven to keep just this side of metaphysics and have penetrated no further than the surface of the coloured tapestry which hides from our eyes the profounder questions of human existence. In doing so I have been aware, I need hardly say, that I have not, in the philosophic sense, been dealing with Time at all, but merely with the awareness of Time, a problem half-psychological, half-sociological, but perhaps none the less absorbing because it does not deal with ultimate reality. I might, I suppose, have called my random imaginings by some such title as "An introduction to the study of the gradual emergence of the time-principle as a dominant factor in the social consciousness". I have preferred to call it, more modestly, the Triumph of Time.

SABLE GODDESS

"Night, sable goddess: from her ebon throne,
In rayless majesty, now stretches forth
Her leaden sceptre o'er a slumbering world."
—*Edward Young*.

SLOWLY, the veil drops. Over fell and moorland the shadows are creeping; and a misty greyness deadens sound. Only the whistling of the shepherd, stumbling down a zigzag path, comes faintly with the wind.

Along suburban streets the lamps jerk into life, while wreathing smoke heralds the evening meal. Here, too, is a certain threat in the approach of winter night; yet there are chinks of light from the abodes of men to give comfort, and the street lamp glimmers helpfully on a damp roadway.

Now the charwoman (dear soul) takes her five shillings with a thankful heart, pulls on the finely feathered hat, and with a steady wheeze makes progress down the garden path. A click at the gate, and the schoolboy is back, savagely hooking his cap to the peg. A short hour, and his father's bowler will hang more decorously beside it.

Nearer the heart of things, coloured lights caper once more before their customers, or spell out the successful play. Humming a snatch from *Cavalleria*, the waiter moves among his empty tables—clinking glasses, folding tall napkins, and assembling knives and forks. Above our heads, aloof from rumbling traffic, topping the high stone buildings, soft grey blends to a dark and peaceful blue.

Once again, it is Night.

·   ·   ·   ·   ·

She is so old, our friend—with her soothing silence and her dark caress. "...Chaos and old Night." Far older and wiser, it seems, than Day—than sun, blue sky, and racing cloud; for though in these things there is perpetual youth, a glorious energy, an elemental force, there can be no lasting peace. Do not be deceived, as you lull yourself in the soft security of a deck-chair; the clouds are creeping up behind you, and they are black with rain.

Her wisdom is contemplative rather than active, it emends and it consolidates—and her cool reason has the purity of the moon, the clear insight of the stars. Night thinks twice where Day thinks once. In the bustle of Day we are carried to and fro in omnibuses, hard-headed men fight for each other's gold, lawyers and rulers of the people converse courteously in richly panelled chambers of council; but in the long hours of Night all is written down, progress is surveyed, and the money locked away. Many the wise afterthoughts scribbled at a bed-side table, many those little points that we had not seen before.

...*And God divided the light from the darkness*. It is written in Genesis. And yet, do you feel it to have been so, yourself? Can you visualise that first morning in terms of black and white, traced down to an ultimate *click* from some divine switch? It is not so to me. Always there was Night, the under-standing, the all-knowing, that sees clearly the thought of all created things—and later there was Day, feeling through the web of Night in the fashion of a million dawns, stretching over the first Heaven with its pale, slim fingers—given us that we might practise the wisdom of Night, as a field that we could sow with the seed of her knowledge.

Yes, she is old—she is from all time. *Darkness was upon the face of the deep. And the Spirit of God moved upon the face of the waters.* Who dares to look without awe into the vault of Night —Night that watched over the Mount of Olives, that saw the army of Nicias in the quarries of Syracuse—Night that gently wrapped the shattered valley of the Somme? In such a pre-sence we bow ourselves low with the knowledge of our futility. We feel as a child that looks up into the face of a kind old man, wondering at each line and wrinkle, awed by that tired look in his sunken eyes—frightened, perhaps, by a pricking little kiss from his stubbly grey beard.

Frightened? Yes, that terror is still to be remembered, though now, in the understanding of the years behind us, it is easy to forget the recurring horrors of our earlier nights. (Charles Lamb did not forget "the hag that nightly sate upon his pillow".) We were not left to ourselves, to sleep and peace, when the light darkened at the bidding of Nurse's finger, and, setting the door the tiniest bit ajar ("*please!*"), she creaked away to crochet in the warm and bright security of the nursery. Then, suddenly, all the host of Evil crowded the little room—in the darkest corners lurked companies of burglars, armed to the teeth and malicious of aspect; murderers bent over the bed, groping for the victim's throat (I could feel warm breath upon my cheek); and, when the wind rattled the fastenings, there were still more of them—rustling the curtains as they climbed quietly in through the open window. Small wonder that a trembling hand reached out for the saving help of electric light—and that a little boy lay back, almost panting with relief, when the familiar objects came up once again for review—the plain white washstand, Rembrandt's "Happy Warrior", the empty fireplace, the crowded book-shelves—seemingly not one whit disturbed. That, perhaps, with one furtive glance under the bed, would be a sufficient reassurance—yet, even after the coming of sleep, the powers of darkness still hung, malignant, over him. There was always the menace of "It".

Down through the vague dim world where men live out their dreams, "It" used to come; something intangible of form or substance, a grey shapeless mass, that crushed out all spark of life as (agony on agony!) it dropped down, ever lower, on to its prey. Only the comforting presence of the whole household could rid me, after great sobbing and screaming, of the awful horror of this thing. Conan Doyle's story of *The Engineer's Thumb* contains the element of "It".

In very early years, a grey rabbit stuffed with straw was my protection and encouragement for the night hours. Then, as I saw more clearly the forces of darkness up against me, electric torches, pokers, pistols and all kinds of bludgeon usurped his kindly counsel. Pity the burglar that blunders on the bedroom of a boy of eight! Thus did we fight the "things that go bump", and even in adult years it is almost possible to trace a reaction against the same latent fear of darkness. The bedside glass of water is the last of the line.

When Night is simply the link between one day and the next, and when those days mean nothing more than

> Little tricycles to ride
> And chocolates with pink inside,

small wonder if "Bed-time, John!" gets a wail of protest, or that successive bursts of "Just another five minutes" bring only tears of rage, a grim hand that pulls, and frantic clutchings at table-leg or door-handle. It does require a little intelligence, a little mental activity in the daytime, to induce the proper appreciation of Night. Besides, the nights are so *long* when you are young.

I pity, and am sorry for, a child's fear of darkness, yet it is natural enough, and implies no criticism of Night itself. Far more deplorable is the low cunning with which the adult mind has sized up the situation. "Do that again, Henry, and Nanny will send you *straight* to bed!" There the child's whole prejudice stands admitted, shamelessly exploited by a fat woman in a white apron. Have children the smallest chance of peace at night when their elders gladly encourage these secret fears, when they are ready to pull down green blinds over the sun, to produce a little Hell out of Heaven—all for their special benefit? I cannot think that they have.

Shame on you, ye nursemaids, and shame, ye mothers of children, that will stand by and see these things done!

Their influence, however, passes; it may even be argued that my personal recollection is that of an acutely "nervous subject". By the age of twelve or thirteen, anyway, Night has become a friend rather than an enemy; the bedroom door can safely be closed without any of the panic of

isolation; and one by one the weapons of war are suffered to
disappear from the bedside table. It is safe to credit something at least to the Public School system—a very complete
and deep-rooted appreciation of the blessings of Night. We
were never more tired than in our school-days; the life was so
active and so incessant, the whirl of it so entirely communal
and completely impersonal, that a little iron bedstead often
loomed, beyond the scurry of the longest day, as the only sure
and strong foundation for existence. It became, within its
narrow confines, a kingdom of the mind—a place, the only
place, where the true values of success and failure in school-
life could be checked and tested, and where one's tiny personal
ego shook itself for a moment free from the monotonous pound-
ing of a great machine. There, while the school clock clangs
out the quarters, while the steady breathing of his companions
rises and falls about him as the swelling of the sea, a boy is for
once immune from the assaults of his little world; to-morrow's
Latin Prose, to-morrow's O.T.C. parade—both have a happy
remoteness in the warm and drowsy security that is a prelude
to sleep. Indeed, at the age of fourteen—when home is four
hours away, when facial characteristics are not imposing,
when meagre athletic attainment gives a handle to the foe—
bed can be a very real asylum.

Such may be the nights of youth, sometimes a little
frightening—always happier, always better understood with
the increase of years; yet in the whole of a lifetime no one
could overcome all Night's mystery, or plumb the infinite
dark depths of our sleeping selves.

> Here we are all by day; by night w'are hurl'd
> By dreames, each one into a sev'rall world.

The thought has not been Herrick's alone, Byron has put it
into very similar words, and both discovered it in Heraclitus
—for the problem of dreams is as old as the world itself. It is,
at first glance, rather a terrifying, even a sinister problem;
it is something that we feel we could never hope to under-

stand; and fundamentally, above all others, it is the obstacle
that makes us distrustful of Night. In the very moment
that I fall asleep I may be chased by foaming negroes along
the Vauxhall Road—though, on the other hand (a preferable
alternative), I may be quietly reading Mrs Molesworth on the
smooth green lawn of a country vicarage.

> And Phansie, I tell you, has dreams that have wings,
> And dreams that have honey, and dreams that have stings. . . .

The possibilities are disturbing, if you survey them in cold
blood; but it is one of the characteristics of a dream that the
most ridiculous incidents appear natural enough—and one
would probably be prepared to accept even the negroes as a
matter of course.

It is a sad mistake, I am sure, to be frightened of dreams;
the worst of them may be reduced to terms of pure indigestion;
and the best—what a world of sensation, triumph and adventure they contain! The dreamer is braver than Hector,
fiercer than Achilles, more handsome than Don John; he is a
finer composer than Wagner, a better painter than Velasquez
—and his intellect is such that it can dazzle continents.
Dreaming, in some vague world beyond time and distance,
the greengrocer corners the cabbage market, and the tram-
driver careers over rails of platinum with a tram of gold.

There is in dreams, someone has said, "a sort of safety-valve
for disappointment"—a kingdom where the deaf can hear,
where the dumb can speak, and where all hopes and longings
see fulfilment. Surely this is one of the blessings of Night?

Do not, for all that, expect too much from your dreams; it
is a mistake to peer at your visions with the pertinacity of an
Old Moore. Splendid things may be done, so Artemidorus
tells us, even by the dreaming of noses. "To dream one has a
fair and great nose is good to all," he says, "for it signifies
subtlety of sense, providence in affairs, and acquaintance with
great personages. But to dream one has no nose signifies the
contrary." Certainly I would not presume to ask you, should

you be granted the happy vision of such a nose, to abandon the hope of "acquaintance with great personages"; yet, should you strike the alternative and have the vital organ conjured away, it would be foolish to rend your garments and give way to grief. Why, completely noseless, your *entrée* into Society would be assured!

Thus can one gibe at the wise old man, but there is little of distinction in the jest. Night holds so many secrets, and who am I to query any arrangements she may have made to cope with the dreaming of noses?—who better than Artemidorus to discover them? Therefore I would urge you, do not swamp these strange prophecies under a full salt-cellar; but taking only the just pinch, go on your way with a respectful awe, remembering always that *Kubla Khan* was written in a dream. While a man dreams, all manner of prophecy, warning, inspiration, hustles his pillowed head, and glimpses otherwise unseen linger in his morning thoughts. "We are somewhat more than our selves in our sleeps," said Browne, "and the slumber of the body seems to be but the waking of the soul."

How sad, Mother Night, that there are so very few who can appreciate you—so many more (among them persons of most estimable character) who view you with suspicion, who frankly fear you—and even those who, seeming to see an improper person, turn the cold shoulder of righteousness upon you. For it has been your misfortune that you bear the brunt of most of our earthly failings—that when the daylight fades, it is your lot to weave a splendid curtain to cloak a host of tragedy and sin; a purity too readily defiled, a solemn confidence too eagerly abused. "Night Life!"—with what a depth of loathing you must hear the phrase, and shudder that your star-hung sky should lend its beauty to such exploitation! —your quiet voice drowned in the moan of the saxophone, your thoughtful hours jerked away by a mass of jostling automata, in the cheap glitter of a *Palais de Danse*. Not for one moment, my dear lady, would I accuse you of prudery (per-

haps I caught your cry of protest?); nor for one moment doubt
there should be wine and song beneath your umbrage—provided only that the revellers are not insensible of the privilege
you confer. One single glance at the heavens, at those white
puffs of cloud scudding over the moon, might prove some consolation; but our only object, in a stuffy crowded room, is to
shut up the windows, to turn on the limelight, and to keep
Night out.

She does her best for *us*, I feel, that we can shine our brightest
when we take our pleasures. On Man, in her great bounty,
she did confer his stiff starched shirt, his coy black tie, those
shyly peeping cuffs—the things that feel so horrid and that
make him look so beautiful; and to Woman she gave those
airy draughty trifles, delicately produced from the inside of
a thick fur coat, like fragile glass unwrapped from tissue
paper, at the appropriate and vital hour.

> Her beauty hangs upon the cheek of Night
> Like a rich jewel in an Ethiop's ear.

Perhaps it may be the feel of our own nightly glory that is
apt to blind us to the beauty of Night itself; yet, though Day
takes all the bouquets, when there is summer sunshine and a
light breeze waving the corn, Night has admirers enough to
whom a rustle from the field-mouse in the long grass, the
trembling of the moon-lit willows, brings its own significance.
It is well to repeat that the test of appreciation for Night ranks
higher than it does for Day, and to him who marches eagerly
down Brighton pier only to push his penny into the machine
marked "What a Night!"—the dark hours offer their message
in vain; for his expectation (though the Edwardian maiden in
her corsets leave it unfulfilled) was not for stars and moon and
sky. Further we will not follow him, as, still hopeful, he
plunges more coppers into neighbouring delights; he is an
object for pity, not for scorn. So, too, we can pity that tall
spinster with the scraggy bun of hair, who peers so intently
into the dark void of the back-garden before she screws up the

window with a determined thoroughness, and lets loose a
torrent of Venetian blind. She is looking, that lady, to see
whether a burglar has climbed the wall from next door, has
landed among the geraniums, and even now creeps through
the "shrubbery" towards the house. ("The Robertsons had
them last week, my dear; one simply can't be too careful.")

To this lady, many other ladies, and some men, Night
means the release of an army of undesirables upon a frightened
world; while their imagination leads them into murky alley-
ways where human rats creep from their holes, muttering
hoarsely among themselves, and one by one slink purposefully
off towards the suburbs. "Night Birds!"—nasty little men
with their scarves tattered, their chins unshaven, and their
photographs at Scotland Yard—they are another curse on
Night; for the riot of nefarious activity is so peculiarly her own
that, should there happen to be a robbery at any other time,
it is so far a curiosity that it must at once be distinguished by
the word "daylight". Whence comes a legend of "dishonest
Night", of "honest Day", and the powers of evil scattered by
the rising of the sun. To this the spirit world makes contribution with those drifting creatures of the half-dark (sad,
frightened, harmless things), creaking the attic staircase on
an endless search for peace—the

> Stubborn unlaid ghost
> That breaks his magic chain at curfew time.

Here is no mystery, other than the tragedy of a deep un-
happiness, no cause for fear save in the contemplation of the
infinite, the unutterable loneliness of an untended soul—and
to him who shrugs a fine shoulder and can laugh his "Non-
sense!" I would urge a little caution (even in so insensitive
a person), that the first shock of discovery may not be too
great; for the outstretched arms of Night stand open to all
things that beg her shelter.

She is the world's Confessor; under her shadow, as beneath
the lofty arches of some great cathedral, we light our candles

and we pray; then the night breeze is the gentle murmur of an organ, the creaking of a branch in the elm blends to the patter of the verger's feet, leading a little party up the aisle—and the cool night air provides a finer incense. What secrets we confide in her!—solemn thoughts too deep to face the light (they might fade beneath the sun)—shy hopes for the future, always more attainable in the unreality of Night—candid confession of a love, of a dependence, for which daytime's familiarity has bred contempt. If through the day we live a life of false-hood, one long pretence of idle conversation that (we are hopeful) has deceived our friends, then only, in the quiet of our room, do we strip off the mask; there he who scoffs at love shows himself the sentimentalist, the psychologist rests his elbows on the window-sill to find his soul reflected in the stars, and the "flippant" jester worries where Day compelled his mockery.

In the prayers of childhood all our relations and especial friends—a gabbled list—we scooped into one huge net, con-fidently upheld for the blessing of Heaven; and though with the added years little of the form of the prayer has changed, our attitude now has a more proper diffidence—and in the result there is more of a hope and less of a demand. The com-forting darkness hears an unembarrassed story, a lingering confession that we dare not trust to Day. "By night an atheist half believes a God."

To each of us his grandest nights, when man and nature seemed to join most perfectly with darkness. This is a feeling I have often known, though one night in the Pyrenees (walking through the little Republic of Andorra) remains the key-note of such recollection. My friend, with greater zeal for explora-tion, had followed the path still further, and I was alone, coming slowly down the mule-track from Ordino, when dusk crept silently over the valley. Then, for a short ten minutes, while the sunshine drained off the hill-tops, while the cool mountain stream sang softly beside me, I seemed to have ap-proached the highest things in life, and to be very near to

God. The purple mist of evening, the barren slopes, the twisting path, and that amazing sense of isolation which comes upon a man in the hills—these were things that seemed, in that short time, to give some clue to the eternal mystery of our creation.

Night fell with one sudden swoop; and all at once (the stream now roaring strangely through a narrow gorge) I was very frightened—so that I ran, stumbling, down the rocky path to Las Escaldas.

The mountains catch the spell of night; dusk in the Berner Oberland, Lauterbrunnen, a gentle whisper from the Staubbach fall—this, too, finds preservation in my memory.

> *Vom Himmel kommt es,*
> *Zum Himmel steigt es,*
> *Und wieder nieder,*
> *Zur Erde muss es,*
> *Ewig wechselnd.*

Night and sleep are great levellers; for while the sun passes comfortably enough through the vita-glass windows of the rich, into the lofty halls of palaces, and gloriously sweeps down on open park-land and on rolling lawn—into that dark little street or shadowed back-yard it fails to make its way; nor does the table of a city clerk brighten beneath its touch. Sun (for all our "lungs of London" and our leisurely slum clearance) remains primarily the privilege of the well-to-do; but Night, making no distinction between rich and poor, sheds its blessing equally over the mansions of noblemen and the three-roomed cottages of their servants. And though the window be too small to catch the sun, it will yet be lar enough for Night, that hides both splendour and squalor beneath the same shroud. Sleep makes no distinction of princes, and in her mercy grants to pride and poverty an equal peace.

Death is a great leveller; for, like Night, she is not to be escaped. "Men fear death as children fear to go in the dark" —but as we learn to love Night, growing old enough to understand, we slowly come to find no fear in Death. After all, each sleep is but a little death, wherein the soul comes nearer to its true existence; and in the same way (as Sir Thomas Browne has observed) that "men sometimes, upon the hour of their departure, do speak and reason above themselves", in sleep, also, we are on a plane above mortality.

Herein lies the essence of Night's mystery, this is a link that binds the living and the dead; in every effort that we make to understand, with each emotion that Night gives, one thought must overshadow all; there is a morning that we shall not see, there is one night from which Man does not wake.

> Sleep is a death; O make me try,
> By sleeping, what it is to die,
> And as gently lay my head
> On my grave, as now my bed.

. . . . . .

A subtle half-light breaks up the eastern sky; chasing the clouds of darkness, forming the clouds of day.

Faintly from the main road comes the squeal of the first tram, and a dog rattles his chain with a drowsy whine.

Rattling alarm-clocks assault the ear, beating through numbed consciousness. Soon, a disdainful maid swishes back the curtains, and Indian tea (libation to the dawn) stands limpid at the bedside. A shapeless form, beneath the counterpane, grunts in hazy recognition of the world. Immense is the superiority complex of an early riser; Cook sets the day in motion as she lights the kitchen fire, and kicks the cat out of a warm basket. First sunlight touches the roof-tops; milk-carts are jolting on the roads; bed-clothes rumple in reluctant haste, while the night shift slouches from the mine.

Again, the rush of life, birds greeting it with morning voice; there is a finger on the button, and the dolls are fully wound.

A sportive breeze rucks up the blind, thrusting a ray of light over the room—and a sick man turns, sighing, with his face to the wall.

For the Night is fled.

GUBBINS ON LOVE

"THAT'LL be Juicy, most like, coming back by way o' Tollard Royal."

"Aye. Plain as a pikestaff. 'Tis the clipperty-clop o' Juicy's dapple mare, new-shod, or I'm a sinner."

Snooper Dodridge and Old Joe Whicher retreated into silence and glared poisonously at Mrs Fotheringay, a stoutish blue-eyed Jezebel, who had come in out of the rain with a nasty yammering whippersnapper. The rest of the company looked more hopefully at their beer: perhaps Juicy would do something to send these gaping wossets packing. 'Twas tarble hard to have two such furriners cluttering up the bar parlour on a Saturday night of all nights, and drinking gin for all the world as though 'twere Michaelmas or Christmas-tide.

"Really, Christopher, this is intolerable: you bring me out into this *bestial* environment, you let the car break down, you abandon it to the care of some incompetent yokel, you bring me in here." The opulent, pigeon-breasted bourgeoise deigned to glance at corduroy and hobnails, winced and stared with exquisite distaste at the shivering cyclist in steaming rain-sodden tweeds who sat staring at a glass of yellow Strong Unnatural Non-intoxicant beside the fire. "And now you tell me I'm drunk. It's *bestial*, Christopher!"

"Dora, for heaven's sake, be quiet: what will these gentlemen think?" Christopher looked round uneasily at the same Saxon stolidity.

"Think? They can't think. You're drunk, Christopher."

"Hush, Dora, please!"

Outside, the rain-streaked night was full of the sound of running water: the runnels, choked and flooded, tugged and foamed at tangled roots and foliage. The hoof-beats slowed to a walk, hesitated, stopped. A blurred patch of light shone for a moment in the window; boots crunched on gravel, then the door opened and Juicy, stooping to dodge the lintel, stood in the muddy threshold puddle. "A ploutering night, Nathaniel. Any room for man and beast?"

"Welcome as flowers in May." Nat Saunders turned to the kitchen and shouted: "Stir yourself there, Tom! Tell Susie to get a bite for Mr Gubbins and dry the blankets. Give the mare a dose of elbow grease yourself. And tell Susie to put her best foot foremost".

A young labourer came in behind Juicy and whispered to him.

"Insulating tape, George? Of course I have." Juicy un-buckled double ulster and tarpaulin, shook rain out of a red untidy beard, and fumbling in deep poacher's pockets, pulled out a dozen objects embedded in a conglomerate of string and wire. The man was built like a traction-engine, but his size was hardly noticeable in a room where everybody had to stoop. He picked out a black coil of gummy tape and George whispered again. Juicy looked at the strangers.

"Body and blood o' Christ!" he said, "It's the Cuddling Curate! And Dora Fluffington! Fine stunt of yours, Wilkins, that protest about cuddling in the public parks. *Exempla docent.* Have another drink: let George propel you into Fordingbridge. Fine driver, George. Drove forty pigs into market only last week. Spring to it, George. Sharp's the word, quick's the action."

George took the insulating tape, tested it with his teeth, and went out. Juicy, in shirt-sleeves, sat down to sliced cold pie and taters. Silence, like an attack of indigestion, settled on the parlour. Mrs Fotheringay carefully preserved a manu-factured smile and Wilkins mumbled sulky greeting. He was a little man (Do you lack Vigour and Self-Confidence?), and thoroughly cowed by Mrs Fotheringay, who now sat, Still Beautiful by Candlelight, watching Juicy Gubbins: from time to time she opened her mouth to speak, but each time she gave up the effort. Mr Wilkins was content not to disturb her. Suddenly she announced, "Maundell What d' y' call him, you know: Maundell Newgate, the nasty little bottle-party journalist, says that you're a poet as well as a philosopher, Mr Gubbins".

"Yes, but wait till I've finished this pie." Juicy shot out, "The trouble is not so much that evil is made a plaything as that playthings are made evil by being mistaken for serious pursuits". Segment by segment the cold pie disappeared. "More beer," he said at last, "quarts all round, and a gallon for yourself, Susie."

The company, mostly farmers and smallholders, were roused to expectation. They had seen Juicy before. "*Cogito ergo* what-not," he said, offering his baccy-pouch to Mrs Fotheringay. "*Nascuntur poetae, fiunt oratores.* I'm a philosopher:

> I often wonder as I go
> What makes the little daisies grow:
> And when I die, as die I must
> And all my bones return to dust,
> Some other fool will want to know
> What makes the little daisies grow.

But a biologist wrote that. To the natterjack or nitwit, the simple unintellectual innocent, immaculate and unthurified, the man like you and me, Mrs Fotheringay, *integer vitae sceleris-que purus*, there can be but one answer——"

The cyclist in the far corner interrupted nervously: "This is rather out of my sphere, but——"

"Spheres in themselves are of comparatively little interest", said Juicy severely. "But a sphere out of itself is no longer self-centred; it is, as it were, decentralised. Music they produce at all times, but their symphonies are silly, their harmonies are hackneyed, and their melodies are muck. Which brings me to the inner heart or nucleus of this disquisition. Tucket. A sound of horns and motors. Enter the Solar System, a polythalamous popsy-wopsy serenely suspended on love alone. On Love, Ladies and Gentlemen.

Gubbins on Love. *De Omnibus Rebus et Quibusdam Aliis.* This, Ladies and Gentlemen, is the Only Animal Endowed by Nature with——.What was I saying? I was attempting what a Very Great Modern Poet has called an oblique presentation of theme. To put it frankly, my attitude, rather than dorsal or ventral, is definitely lateral. The theme never appears in explicit statement. It is formulated through a series of complex metaphors which defy a paraphrasing of the sense into an equivalent prose. *Per jocum et saltum, per quantum et quintum, obscurum per obscurius,* as another modern poet says, *ad aspidistra. Natura non facit saltum?* Not a bit of it. Take Bohr, take Planck, take Dirac, Heisenberg, Stern-Gerlach, One-legged Winnie and the Intelligent Reading Public, and what have you? Nothing. Penetratable impermanence replaces permanent impenetrability. Man makes matter, matter makes mind, mind makes man. Reversible adiabatic cycle. Man doesn't matter, matter doesn't mind, mind won't man the boat and we shan't be home to-night. Take atoms, take protons, take the querulous quantum. Nature, Ladies and Gentlemen, may be regarded as a Cheshire cat, or, more profoundly, as a cat on hot bricks, starring the observer, even the well-known and amiably disposed Stanley McBaldwin, in the capacity of hot brick."

Susie brought in the beer and a large hunk of Blue Vinney, and Juicy, passing the ridge or summit of his discourse, graduated into silence.

Under his mellowing verbiage an undergrowth of conversation had already sprouted: the cyclist, pop-eyed and gaping, dared not speak again, but Mr Wilkins was whispering to Mrs Fotheringay, and a young chap from Bottlebush was playing up to Smiler Brown, the Cranbourne wag. "Ole Bill's bin an gone and got one of them glass eyes, he has."

"Has he now?" asked Smiler. "Well, I reckon as how I wouldn't trust meself wi' one. I lay I'd feel as how what I were seeing weren't natural."

"Arn on 'ee know Holton Heath?" Old Gossip Batey

asked. "Talk o' growing mangolds down there. Mangolds for to make alcool, they do."

A burst of laughter greeted this bit of news. "Alcool for to drive motors and suchlike."

The laughter doubled. Susie distributed the beer.

"Mangolds take all the natur out o' the soil", said Joe Whicher in walled-eyed meditation. "Holton Heath at that! There's a power o' good in slag and artificial, but miracles, as I allus says to Mary, be miracles, and tarblish difficult, and it baint no use fer you nor I to try 'em."

"I 'low as how some o' they young fellers up to Lunnon is a bit queer in the head. There baint no alcool in any mangolds as I've ever met, or they hoggets of mine would be dead sozzled-out this living minute."

Mrs Fotheringay started to giggle, and hastily checked herself. She felt sick.

"Christopher. This is indecent, bestial", she said. "I feel ill. Put your arm round me."

"Dora, please be quiet: I'll take you away soon."

"You don't love me. I know you don't. How can you be so cruel? Last night you said——"

"Dora!"

"You said—", Mrs Fotheringay, skidding past tears, pulled up at indignation.

"You said you really did believe in cuddling. You said it was a Christian duty and we should not be ashamed."

"Dora!!"

"You said it was axiomatic."

Juicy, reaching for the cheese, stopped to elucidate: "Axioms in philosophy are not axioms till proved upon our senses. Mr Wilkins isn't in his senses to-night. At least, not in the sense or senses that he evidently was last night. Wait till I've finished this Blue Vinney".

"'Tis a great subject, is pigs", Smiler Brown was saying. "There's old Mooty 'Oodgate. Says I to him this morning, I says, if you wants pigs, real pigs, from dthick 'ee old zow,

I call tell 'er where five bob'll do it. Ped-ee-gree Large Black
he be, and a regular bone-shaker at that. Bust me, but didn't
young Tom laugh! Laughed like a jellyfish. A regular boneshaker, I says...."

They roared in sympathy—a regular boneshaker, Copper-
nob's old boar a regular boneshaker, and him no better than
a hog! A regular boneshaker! That was real het.

Juicy washed down the last chunk of cheese, stretched his
legs, leaned back and, judging his distance, opened fire:
"Pigs", he said, "is a great subject, but as that daring sceptic
Dr Watts observed: 'When a subject is proposed to your
cogitations, consider first whether it be knowable at all or no'.
Take bricks or take sawdust. Sawdust is knowable. But why?
Because you know what you want to do with sawdust. You
know what you want to know——"

"Pigs is like women", put in Tom Hoddinot.

"Aye", said Snooper Dodridge.

Mrs Fotheringay shuddered.

"Not ladies," said the man from Bottlebush, "ladies is
highbred."

"Aye. Ladies is hybrid. Some be and some baint", said
Smiler.

"Sawdust", Juicy went on, "is a great subject, a knowable
subject, scobology. We lift, move, burn and trample sawdust.
Hence the pyramids; no, the percepts; no, I mean the essential
concepts: recurrent situations, impenetrability, space, heat,
mass. Our desires are simple, mechanical, and simple our
corresponding science. But is porcology a subject? And if
pigs, are women? And will the architypical concepts serve?
We lift, move, burn and trample women. Good; women a
branch of scobology. We feed, fondle, fatten and fight for
women. Excellent. Women a branch of porcology. And then?
No action. Therefore, no concept. The intrinsic nothing,
stark tautology, irrelevant, the essence: *De omnibus rebus et
quibusdam aliis*—Love. But if no concept, is love a subject?
What do we want to do with love? Lift it, move it, burn it,

tread in it? Halve it? No, have it. Let it be. No action. Therefore no concept, no amatory science; mere anecdote, pure poetry, and the rest—porcology.

> Grotesquely in the open light
> Digits and limbs gesticulate,
> And blinds go rattling up the sky,
> That fell last night, precipitate.

And as another Very Great Poet has observed:

> I waive the quantum o' the sin,
> The hazard o' concealin';
> But och it hardens a' within,
> And petrifies the feelin'.

In the words of yet another, and more modern, V.G.P., 'the wages of sin is sausages'."

"Juicy," said the man from Bottlebush, "the lady looks faint."

Mrs Fotheringay pulled herself together: "Not at all," she said, "this is a very interesting subject".

"All subjects which are non-existent are interesting", said Juicy. "In the words of the inimitable Descartes *Aut sum, aut non sum, ergo sum*, whence non-existence is a fundamental reality of the philosophic imagination. It occludes existence, itself a part of itself. It is twice blessed. It blesseth him that is and him that aint. Its loveliness increases not, but droppeth as the gentle Jew from heaven, on man's first disobedience and the fruit, the ripe Newtonian pippin. But we digress. I take it that you object——" Juicy stared aggressively at Old Joe Whicher, who had just lifted his tankard. Joe hesitated and put it down again.

"No," he said thoughtfully, after wiping his mouth with the back of his hand, "No, I don't object, not at my time of life Mr Gubbins. It's been a mortal bad year fer turnip though."

"You object," Juicy insisted, "that there are sciences which are purely contemplative. Nay. No go. *Nego. Non probare protestis.* The concept defines the conditions of a preparation, a possible action. Contemplation, however disinterested, is

the study of potential action: it is the empirical extrapolation
of kinaesthetic sensation; it is extensive, hypothetical. Whereas
Love——"

"Yes?" Mrs Fotheringay seemed to be recovering. She
looked up from the small mirror in her handbag and smiled.

"The beer's flat", said Juicy. "Broach another barrel,
Susie, and draw a sample quart for Old Joe Whicher and a
double gin for Mr Wilkins."

"How's young George getting on with that-there motor?"
said Snooper.

"Like a wooden clock with the wheels on fire", said
Nathaniel. "It'll be right as rain inside ten minute."

Christopher dragged himself out of his melancholia. "I
sometimes think——" he said.

Juicy nodded. "I know," he said kindly, "we were all
young once."

"I think——"

"I'm sure you do. My old grandmother——"

"That the categories——"

"Exactly. My old grandmother——"

"Damn your grandmother. I sometimes think——"

"So you say", put in Old Gossip Batey, finishing his beer.
"So you say."

"My grandmother. I mean, I sometimes think——"
Christopher swallowed his gin and spluttered like a lump of
heated chlorate. "The category——"

"The question is," said Juicy, "are grandmothers ultimate
human values or not. Are grandmothers——"

"The category of grandmothers——" Christopher began.

"That", persisted Juicy, "is the question. Zusammen-
setzung, in one of the most profound adumbrations which has
ever darkened the farthest horizons of the baffling human
mind, asserts——"

"The category——"

"Or rather, tentatively hypothesises an *umlaut* or *ersatz* in
the general predicate, whereas Kummerbund——"

"The cat——"

"Virtually denying the principle of the excluded middle, postulates a negative issue *per se*, in which case——"

"The cat——"

"Rhenic hypothemes interpolate adestral, or rather, pneumic astypulation, so that——"

"The cat——"

"Paradictically speaking, a lutupic pnem or imbal may be——"

"Or may not be. The cat——"

"Including the cat. And anyway you can look it all up in the *Solipsist*, Vol. xxxix, iii, 399 (Supp. 3); Nathaniel, what's the time? I feel ill—touch of lumbago and spotted fever I'm afraid. Perhaps a little more beer—But no. What's that? The clock's stopped? That's nothing, I'll mend it: I know all about grandfather clocks, I kept a hundred and thirty-seven white mice in one."

Juicy detected signs of scepticism and turned his battery on the cyclist. "It's a fact, sir, I've been most things in my time: pianist, fisherman, inventor and hedonist, linoleum, gold-dust, actuary, architect, anarchist, colonel and kangaroo-tails. Were you ever a burglar, sir? What's that, Nathaniel? Ten-thirty? Aye, as you say, might as well be hung for a sheep as for a lamb. Remember that crate you bought at Blandford? Cap D'Or or I'm a sinner. A curious drink, but bring it up. Mrs Fotheringay. A glass? Two glasses? A tumbler? Brace of tumblers, Nat."

"Of course I see your point, Mr Gubbins," said Christopher, "and often I find myself in these mazes too. Does a high degree of mental activity, I ask myself, necessarily lead to abstraction and introspection? You say they are separate but it seems to me that they are in practice devilish involved. The abnormal development of the higher centres, necessary at times if we are to manipulate the complex system by which we keep an artificially large population alive in a small area, leads, at the times when that sensibility is not needed, to a

morbid feeling of futility. Consider the sensibility of the intelligent reading public; think how a tiger, deprived of the
necessity of struggling for existence, becomes miserably
neurotic. Perhaps the only solution is to get drunk when
we're not working."

"But take Beethoven, take Shakespeare, take Plato, take
Goethe, take Newton, take Spinoza——"

"Aye," said Old Joe Whicher ominously, "take Spinoza."

"Take Rabelais, take Schopenhauer, take Luther, take
Benedictine. There you have it. Benedictine. Benedict.
Hence the soul cannot be possessed of the divine union until
it has freed itself of the love of created beings. In the words
of a Very Great Modern Poet: *Mulier modo mulier sed cigara
bona fumigatio est.*"

"Of course, there's the psychoanalytic method. In spite of
all your rot about the non-existence of amatory subject, it is
possible to get rid of all sorts of complexes and inhibitions and
so place your affections where you can get what you want."

"Porcology, science of getting what you want, *i.e.* getting
what desires you want. Related to love about as much as a
troat to a travelling trocar."

"Well, look at me. I've got rid of a whole mass of repressions and inhibitions. I go straight out for what I want.
I get it."

"And a damn lot of good it is to you. The wages of sin is
sausages. Were you ever in love? You were probably as
miserable as hell one minute and as happy as a sand-boy the
next. Or maybe you were miserable all the time. But you
were alive, and you knew that it was good to be alive."

Christopher wavered for a moment. "I don't admit it," he
said; "you'll agree that it is good to get rid of repressions?"

"I dunno," said Juicy thoughtfully, tasting the Cap D'Or,
"I rather like a certain amount of repression myself. It's
more fun and it gives you all sorts of motives for acting and
for living, and that's more than your analysis will do."

"Well, it's only beginning, and anyway it does, often, give

free play to motives that have been checked and obscured. In time it may go further. The sensibility of the intelligent reading public——"

"Stay thine obstetric hand, and damn the I.R.P. What is analysis? A process of taking to pieces a bad poem that exists in the patient's mind. What's poetry? A process of putting in a better one. In the words of the great three-tailed Bloomsbury Bashaw, the esemplastic imagination is the goods. There is a logic of the imagination as well as a logic of concepts. If you want to make people feel the value of this, that or the other you'll have to put it into poetry: poetry, mind you, not verse. Take Shakespeare. Or, better still, take Gubbins— Have some more opiate?" Juicy filled up the glasses and went on. "There's the temptation of St Antony for example. This sort of thing:

> Bucolic bacchanals delight
> To scandalize the anchorite:
> Strabismal glaucous optics bulge
> Where solecistic sylphs indulge
> In flagrant impropriety.
> Frenetic phanerogamy
> By universal knowledge is
> More potent than exegesis
> To mitigate nimiety
> Of such austere austerity.

Or if you prefer the unadorned simplicity of Shepherd's Bush or Mayfair to the *persicos adparatus*, the polysyllabic dissonance of Bloomsbury or Majorca, try this:

> I had read mathematics
>   And words of the wise,
> I had studied the classics
> And pure mathematics,
> Economics, aesthetics,
>   But looked in your eyes
> And forgot (in italics)
>   *The words of the wise.*

Consider for a moment——"

"Look here," said Wilkins, "why the devil don't you

publish stuff like that first one. It would go like blazes with the left-wingers."

"Of whom there are fifty-two, all leaders of the movement and too broke to buy each other's books. Ask Kleinfeld. And anyway they get review copies. Now when I write——"

"You write for posterity, don't you, Mr Gubbins?" said Mrs Fotheringay quite sincerely. By some non-Euclidean route she had now regained sobriety, though she had, of course, lost herself in the process.

"Interlocution, that's my object, as integration might be that of a mathematician. A poem properly interlocuted is a theorem proved, an autocephalous prolepsis, a verbal pattern gubbinised, ecstatically infixed, contemporaneously unique. I adopt presentive pretermission, sybilline symbols. My poems are concentrated, inspissated and coagulated sense. They look and feel like igneous conglomerates. They taste like india-rubber. They smell——"

Wilkins made an effort at frivolity. "Exactly", he said.

"You have it," Juicy continued, "they smell exactly. They have a geometric pungency, an acrid incontortability. You don't need to read them: taut pronouns shriek on resinous adjectives, adverbs are quivering rockdrills, shrill verbs grind nouns to a screeching dental edge. Neotectonic multi-loquence, stentorophonic resonance, re-amplified oscillation, pulsating walls and bridges, fulminating trumpets. Downfall of Mussolini, revolution in Madagascar, Late Wire from the Course, discovery of the Missing Link, heavy-weight boxer's come-back, squaring of the circle by A. R. Orage, Pelion on Ossa, Gubbins on Love. That, roughly speaking, is the way one of my poems works. I speak subject to correction, of course."

"Aye, that's what I says", Snooper Dodridge put in truculently. Like the others, he had been overawed by the Cuddling Curate and the awful Mrs Fotheringay but not by Juicy's rhetoric, for beyond all doubt Juicy was mad, though what he didn't know about pigs weren't worth knowing.

"I reckon as how young George ought to have finished fiddling with that-there engine hours ago."

"Came in ten minutes ago by the back way and the car's as right as a trivet. I reckon he'll be dry as a bone now." Nathaniel raised his voice, but Wilkins was too busy to hear.

"Grant your point," he said to Juicy, "but aren't you over-looking——"

"It seems to me", Mrs Fotheringay interrupted, "that you're forgetting——"

"I know it," said Juicy, "I knew it when I started, you're going to mention Lawrence, the wrong Lawrence, the man who tied his lumbar ganglions round his solar plexus to keep his metaphysics warm. Well, give me Intellect as Bill Blake used to say. I don't mind a spot of Katharsis now and then, but none of this hunting bugbears with a bowie knife. The average woman has two and a quarter children, and, what with the washing and the measles and the Education Officer, quite enough too. Perhaps I digress, but in the words of Mrs Gummidge: Poetry matters little to the modern world; those who care about it can only go on caring. Vich likevise is the end of all things. Pluck tufted Crow-toe, and pale Jessamine, the I.R.P. is dead, diseased or daft. In the words of one of the greatest of V.G.M.P.'s, Deshil Holles Eamus. Deshil Holles Eamus. Hoopsa, boyaboy, hoopsa! Ladies and gentlemen: let me recapitulate——" Juicy was losing his grip: twitters of conversation had broken out here and there among his audience and the man from Bottlebush was furtively shuffling a pack of cards. Old Gossip Batey grumbled to Ned Cooper: "Bëath? What do them gert boys want wi' a bëath? I aint never had a bëath but once in me life, an' then I ketched a cold".

Juicy sucked at his pipe for a moment, and Wilkins seized his opportunity: "But surely Lady Chatterley is a convincing proof that——"

"Little boys should be obscene but not absurd." Juicy resumed. "Let us consider this psychological rhetoric in the

light or lunar radiation of rhetorical psychology. The
Aesthetiken of Plotzenhoffer, is, approximately, a sublima-
tion of the subliminal appetencies of the spiritual ego. It is
tripe——" The audience stared—"It is tripartite in its
nature. It is, in fact, Plastikon, and therefore subject to the
vernal and autumnal equinoxes". The company gave a gasp
of relief. They had doubted his ability to overcome the awful
difficulty which, they felt, was lurking somewhere hereabouts.
Juicy went on with a magnificent gesture: "Let me extend
my method. It opens up infinite vistas of a microscopic
analysis of the macrocosm. Consider the famous 'Ode to a
Blood-orange':

> Thou oblate spheroid of the gayest hue,
> Thou slowly ripening product of the sun,
> Sweeter thou art than Burton's brew,
> Thy praise is endless though my song is done.

"Observe", he said, "the tender beauty of these lines, so
reminiscent of Keats at his best. Note the use of the formal
elements to produce a tone in keeping with the sentimental
appeal; mark the quiet beat of the rhythm as the stanza pro-
gresses: observe the awakening and linking of the powerful
emotional groups connected with colour, sunshine, sweetness,
Beer. It is in this that the main psychological value of the
poem lies. It satisfies the appetency, the desire to combine
certain groups or emotions, and this union possesses that
permanency which is the common characteristic of all good
art. Again, the satisfaction is not obtained at the expense of
some other appetency, as happens, unfortunately, with certain
specialist poets, such as Mr de la Mare. Such work can be of
no permanent value.

"Observe, too, the calm dignity, tinged with regretfulness,
at the close. The poet feels the inadequacy of words to convey
his feelings. He can do no more....Yet, by the beauty of his
verse he has succeeded in the great object of all poetry, indeed
all art—Communication. He has induced in the reader an
emotional complex, similar to that the poet must have him-

self experienced when he first saw, with the poet's eye, a blood-orange".

"Blood-oranges", said Old Joe Whicher, "is queer things, I mind the time when——"

"You're right," said Juicy with conviction, "you're right. The mills of God grind slowly for they know not what they do. There is a tide in the affairs of women which, taken at the flood, leads God knows where. Take Helen, take Cleopatra, take Heloise, take Messalina or Louise Labé, take Sappho or Mrs Wilcox, take Mrs Gummidge, take yourself——"

"Aye, take yourself," mumbled Gossip Batey, looking at his beer as though it were the end of the world, "take yourself."

"And where are you? Where is your virtue. Where is your central pattern, your fundamental rhythm? Read Plato, read Aristotle, read Schopenhauer, Fracastorius, Bradshaw. The average woman has two and a quarter children. *Ubi dolor, ubi digitus*, one must needs scratch where it itches. England expects—But no. One touch of nature makes the whole world sin; and pigs, as my esteemed friend Smiler has observed, is a great subject. To that I would offer only one suggestion: pigs is pigs. Or shall I say, with my more learned but no less esteemed friend Professor G. E. Moore, that if I compare the bare hypothesis that the proposition 'pigs is pigs' is true (which I will call the identity theory) with the bare hypothesis that it is false, I certainly get the impression that the arguments against the hypothesis that the identity theory is true are somewhat weaker than the arguments against the hypothesis that the identity theory is false. Whilst not contending that it is anywhere near certain that the identity theory is true, I may say quite definitely that I am against the view that the arguments for its falsity are at all considerably stronger than those in favour of its truth. *Mulier modo mulier, laetitia perfecto est*. Take Wilkins."

There was a pause. Everybody expected Juicy to go on. It sounded as though the clock had stopped, but no, it was still ticking, tick-tock, tick-tock. Juicy slowly refilled his pipe.

Young George had come in from the kitchen and was waiting. Mrs Fotheringay looked doubtfully at Gubbins.

"Take Wilkins", he said. "Try the Queen's Head, good sound beds, none of those woggling cast-iron quadrupeds. If there's one thing I hate more than another, it's an accompaniment that sounds like the shorthand-typing of the recording angel."

Mrs Fotheringay woke up. "Juicy," she said, "I may call you Juicy, may I not? I want you to do something for me. I want you to see me home."

"But Dora!" Christopher sat up and looked at her in horror. "You have to come to the Schnitzelbaum's to-morrow."

"I don't care. What was it Mr Gubbins said? *Mulier modo mulier?* It was noble of you, I know, Juicy, but if you knew how I thought of you all these months. These long, dreary, months——"

"Dora," said Juicy, "*Non sum qualis eram.* Take me for all in all, you will not look upon my what-is-it again. And besides, if I don't mend the old sow's sty to-morrow, she'll eat a mile o' turnips some fine night."

"Do you mean to suggest——"

"Come on, Dora! This chap says the car's all right now. Come on."

"Aye," said Old Joe Whicher under his breath, "come on."

Assisted by Wilkins, Mrs Fotheringay came on. She was fat, and she was more than a little drunk, but she walked to the door with something of a gentleman's dignity. She was a woman and she had been alone for most of the evening in a shabby, stuffy, beer-house with a dozen boors and two men who should have known better.

"Good-night," she said, "Good-night—Juicy. Remember that we too are sometimes——" she hesitated, then added: "Good-night, Good-night." She went out and stumbled over the doorstep.

"*Sic transit gloria feminae*", the cyclist ventured.

"Women are funny creatures", said Juicy, without bothering to correct him. "They are the only animals (with the exception of cats) which have a preliminary period of excitement after morphia, for example: the average woman has two and a quarter——"

"Aye, so you say, so you say", said Old Gossip Batey doubtfully.

"One of the most remarkable things about woman——" the cyclist began.

"Young man," said Juicy severely, "generalisation is damnation. The average woman——"

"Well I never met one as did," Joe Whicher said.

"Joe, you've said it. Woman is a percept, not a concept: the raw material of art, not science, and in art, as in racing, form is the thing."

"I say," said Wilkins, sidling into the room again, "have you seen Dora's handbag anywhere? It's rather important."

Nathaniel perfunctorily searched the room. "If we find it we'll send it over first thing in the morning", he said, emptying a spittoon into the fireplace.

"No: we must have it to-night. I mean——"

George came in from the lane. "The lady says it's all right," he announced, "she says she put them in her suit case with your spare braces."

"And that reminds me," said Nathaniel, who had been in the kitchen doing some careful calculations with a wet finger on the bench, "eleven-and-tuppence sir, including young George."

Wilkins searched his pockets. "I must have left my notecase outside." "Worse come to worse, I'll flap the dimmock myself," said Juicy helpfully, but Wilkins went out and returned with the money.

"Beating in the cinnamon while the galleon's in Jamaica?" Juicy asked.

"What's that?" said Wilkins, turning round suddenly and banging his head on the lintel. "O damnitall, damnitall,

damnitall. Good-night gentlemen, damn you", he glared at Joe Whicher and went out, slamming the door.

"And you say he's a parson, do you?" asked Joe Whicher aggressively. "Wants spanking, the nasty little runt. Night-walking rakehells, I call 'em. And as for she.... If my old 'ooman——"

"Sharp words never slice turnips", said Nathaniel. "Custom is custom, though I'd as lief be poor as a church mouse and keep a decent house than live like a fighting-cock and own the sort o' place such highflown vermin patronise. Though I'm sure there's no offence meant if they be friends o' yourn, Mr Gubbins."

"Takes all sorts to make a world", said the man from Bottlebush.

"The world being the totality of existent sorts, you're probably right, or at any rate tautological, which is probably the same thing. But——" Juicy shrugged his shoulders and started to fill a pipe.

"Gentlemen, I'm mortal sorry if they folks have spoiled a friendly evening", Nathaniel interpolated. "But what's the use of sitting here like a dying duck in a thunderstorm? Susie! Bring beer for the house. Perhaps Mr Gubbins will talk to us."

"He aint done nothing else yet", said an old man with whiskers.

"Logic is one kind of obviousness, there's no sharp line between your poetry and logic. *Natura non facit saltum sed homo aliter non potest*. Yet maybe as many people see the poetic pattern as the logical." Juicy seemed to be talking to himself. "For there is a pattern about things that isn't reasonable: the right things happen at the right time always, if you've the wit to notice. But you've got to knuckle down to it," he went on, raising his voice a little, "and that's like building a massive world on gyrostatic nothing. To be honest with yourself until your world's intrinsic mass and motion holds it firm, down to the immaterial dark, the central point.—Take funerals," he said, still following his tortuous lucubrations, "why are funerals such fun? Because they aren't. Why are mothers-in-law? Because they aren't. You can't go through furze without mokins. You remember Ted Cockles who deserted the widow Tonks? I don't, but it reminds me of fishing. Both in human and in piscatorial or piscine affairs the best of flies is apt to conceal a hook, and Satan finds some mistress still for idle hands to woo. Does not Gilbert White say in his Fifty-third epistle to the honourable Baines: 'Some young men went down lately to a pond on the verge of Wolmer Forest to hunt flappers'. *Mais ou sont les neiges d'antan?*

> When he well dronken had with wine
> Then would he speke no word but Latine.

Frigidus in montis canis liquescit humor. A cold dog makes water on the mountain, *humor*, by way of a joke. *Et in Arcadia ego.... Nunc ab angulo....O lente, lente, currite noctis...*down to the cold *post coitum, homo tristis.* Drinking will quench the longest thirst, but work and sharp latinity, praise God, will mend it."

Juicy swallowed about a pint and a half of beer to clear his throat. The others also fortified themselves with drink. The old man with whiskers spat viciously.

"'Vanity of vanities', said Sir Richard Grenville and did not stay for an answer. What is man but a jilted jackanapes fishing Minkowskian waters for the old Platonic tiddlers, a gibbering egopompous puppet following the involuted intricacy of the intrinsically unattainable, the ineffable ideal, and ever seeking to escape the thundering rattle of the can that blunders at his tail, the can that is, the caudal cause, the imponderable past, the ever-present future, implied potentiality, simple and pure Existence? Slower than continental drift, slower than the great McBaldwin's brain, he ploughs the inky firmament and sees, beyond Protagorean bluff and past the gin and Stygian bitters we call life, the roar and clatter of eternity. In the words of the very greatest of V.G.M.P.'s, 'What is actual is actual only for one time',

for what is true is true only for one man, and without
man the notion of impossibility would be impossible. *Sub-
lata cauda, tollitur effectus*. But woman! Woman! O mystic
might, O marvellous mechanism! Like a bedbug or a complicated Orrery she goes all wrong but gets there. Everything she sees she wants and everything she wants she seizes.
Therefore we happy underconstumblers and transmogrifiers
of the absolute absolve all them that truly invent and un-
feignedly digest the sword of universal brotherhood, leaving
joy and felicity inexcruciably intermingled and sense and
non-sense making one single hyper-music as before. But I,"
said Juicy with a noble gesture, banging his empty tankard
on the bench, "I am the universal observer, the I.R.P.,
Cogito ergo cogito, and that's that. Being has been my business
since boyhood—batrachiae and barristers, bigamy and bull-
frogs, barratry and barprops, ballyrags and balderdash, and
the greatest of these is Charity. Faith, Hope, Charity, and
Mathematics, the Trinity of Virtues. Bring more beer and
let us contemplate existence. It has been said that non-
existence is a fundamental reality of the philosophic imagination. Recognition of the existence of a condition implies
recognition of the possibility (in an abstract sense) of the non-
existence of the condition. If non-existence is impossible, then
existence is meaningless and we are where we were, up the
pole. As it says in the great *Principia Chaotica*: If the beginning
of existence began at the beginning of the existence of non-
existence, then existence did not exist prior to the beginning
of the existence of non-existence, otherwise its existence would
have been non-existent before the beginning of the existence
of non-existence and therefore its existence would have been
non-existent. But antedate the existence of non-existence by
three days and where are you? Its existence begins before
the beginning of existence and this pre-existent existence is
existent before existence. Existence is then non-existent and
non-existence is existent, the beginning of existence being
non-existence, showing the existence of non-existence under

non-existent circumstances and the non-existence of existence under existent circumstances. If, however, the beginning of existence is non-existent——"

The company stirred uneasily. The rain had stopped.

"Put a sock in it", said the old man with whiskers.

"Put several socks in it", said Juicy. "Neo-Procrustean bottles for non-Euclidean wine. If thy nose offend thee, hypothecate its non-existence. In the words of Ludovicus Cantabrigiensis: What cannot be said, cannot be said. I homologate, I do indeed. The expression of our thought is bound within the mesh of language. *Eppur si muove, si muove.* AND HOW!"

SKETCHES FROM EXPERIENCE

THE RETURNED TRAVELLER Peter Fleming
FALL IN, GHOSTS   Edmund Blunden

THE RETURNED TRAVELLER

THE flying fish scuttled out from under our bows, which forged implacably, and with a brisk munching sound, through the small blue waves. The Portuguese ventriloquist in the steerage, a tall fierce man, began to pace the deck below me in a methodical way; he walked many miles in the course of the next three weeks. The sub-continent which we had left at dawn was now no more than a thin drab smudge where the sky joined the sea. I was going home again.

The lunatic, asked why he persistently battered his head against the wall of his cell, replied: "It's so marvellous when you leave off".

The Pleasures of Life are mostly like that: I mean the recognised Pleasures, like Dancing, and Reading Worth While Books, and Beagling, and Brilliant Conversation—the recognised Pleasures, not the liberties we take with our freedom. This is particularly true of the English, whose relaxations may be regarded more as Tests of the National Character than as anything else. But its truth is seldom admitted. It needed the courage and the percipience of lunacy to draw up an accurate emotional balance-sheet, whereon the greatest, indeed the only asset was shown to be the cessation of voluntarily sustained liabilities. "It's so marvellous when you leave off...."

It applies, as I say, to almost all our deliberate attempts to make life less intolerable. If you doubt me, stand in the streets at night and observe the faces of the revellers as, sinking back into a taxi, they light their first cigarette after quitting some place of entertainment, whether public or private. You will see there a real joy, something far purer and deeper than the spasmodic and perfunctory gleams of satisfaction which have chased themselves (or, more probably, been chased) across the revellers' features in the course of the evening. "It's so marvellous when you leave off." For the sake of such blissful relief it was almost worth beginning.

If this be true (as it undoubtedly is) of those brief, those almost surprise attacks on happiness—those hopes on which, duty and custom forbidding us to recognise them as forlorn, we waste the fag-end of a day—how much truer should it be of more protracted campaigns on wider fields for the same reward. Of Travel, for instance. Travel is, or passes for, one of the Pleasures of Life. Looking out over the tedious azure sea, I asked myself, not for the first time, whether the lunatic's formula holds good for Travel.

A year ago I should have said that it did; I should have said so without any reservations at all. A year ago, as the aeroplane sang westward through the warm air along a desolate coast, it seemed to me that there could be nothing to qualify the delights of return. But now——

All the way back after your first long journey, you feel (like the reveller escaping in his taxi-cab) a very real pleasure. And this pleasure—unlike his—is cumulative; it grows rather than diminishes as you get nearer home. Almost you recapture that most memorable of raptures, the End of Term Feeling: that wonderful emotion whose growth to ecstasy was not only assured, but could be followed, charted, and rejoiced in, like Mustard and Cress or the Batting Averages. Paying your last hotel bill is like showing up your last examination paper. You throw a now useless handful of foreign currency into the sea with the same careless and magnificent gesture with which, years ago, you flung a celluloid protractor into the fire. When you pack your suitcase for the last time you bring to this no longer serious task something of that spirit of vigorous parody with which you sang the hymn at the last Prayers of term. This time to-morrow where shall I be?...

Your journey is at an end; and however much you have enjoyed it you are glad. In this world the desire to escape is for ever being reborn, the fugitive's sense of direction always changing; unconscious of bathos, the gaol-bird nips back into prison with a profound sense of release.

So the end of your first journey is probably the best part of it. On the horizon before you there are no clouds. The value of native things has been enhanced by separation; their faults are all forgotten. You look forward with a keen delight to slipping back once more into those surroundings whose cloying and oppressive familiarity drove you away. It is lovely to be home again, you think. Naturally: for you do not know as yet what a dreadful thing it is to be a Returned Traveller.

Poor innocent, you even like the prospect. You hope that separation will have enhanced your value, too, in the world to which you are returning. Even if you have accomplished nothing, even if you have scamped or missed all the sights worth seeing, you have at least been there and back; and you cannot help knowing that an account, however bald, of doings, however ordinary, acquires a certain *ex officio* glamour or impressiveness by reason of the fact that they were done at a distance. You think with satisfaction of the exotic galaxy of labels which stars your luggage, of the curious things which it contains, of the stories you will have to tell....

The stories you will have to tell.... The English language is too often ambiguous. There are two possible meanings to that sentence, but in your innocence you overlook the other one, the one which conveys compulsion, the one which ought to end "whether you like it or not".

It is natural that you should overlook it. You have never before played the Returned Traveller; you have no reason to suspect how tedious and shameful a rôle this is. But once you have played it you can never forget its peculiar humiliations.

Watching the Portuguese ventriloquist thunder purposefully up and down his narrow beat as we crawled across the seas towards Lisbon, I knew that it was the memory of these humiliations which qualified my delight in returning, which threatened the validity of the lunatic's formula, which made it less marvellous than it ought to have been to leave off. In

three weeks, I thought, I shall be once more a Returned
Traveller, and I recalled with a horrible clarity the incon-
veniences of that position.

At first you rather enjoy it. It seems after all, when you
come to put your experiences into words, that your journey
was not so uneventful as you had thought. There is really a
great deal to tell, and you enjoy telling it, the first time. In
your narrative the longueurs are left out, the contretemps
acquire dramatic value, disappointments and disasters lose
their power to rankle and become merely good jokes at your
own expense. Your family and your closest friends make
sensible and appreciative audiences; it is not until you have
been back perhaps a week that your stock of travellers' tales
become a burden of which you would willingly be rid.

Its market value remains high: much too high. It is true
that people appear anxious to hear what you saw and did.
But how much of their curiosity is mere politeness? You become morbidly obsessed with the fear of being a bore; and in
a very short time you are one, to yourself. The recital of your
experiences, which you now find so distasteful and oppressive,
must surely irk your listeners too? Inevitably it has crystal-
lised into a series of set pieces; those happy phrases which you
coined in the first flush of homecoming adorn it still, un-
welcome, stale, but serviceable relics, like the Christmas cake
which haunts the tea-table far into January. With a cold and
growing horror you listen to your own voice parading this
redundant sequence of well-chosen images and epithets which
have long lost their spontaneity and, with their spontaneity,
the justification for their choice. In your own eyes you stand
convicted as a cheapjack.

But there is no escape. You have to go on hawking your
wares. You are caught between the Scylla of garrulity and the
Charybdis of reticence; you must make up your mind whether
it is better to be known for an active or a passive bore, for you
cannot shun the reproach of being tedious by being tongue-
tied. If you respond to the Desdemona-like importunacy of

hostesses—"Oh yes," people will say, "he's been to Ultima Thule; and by God, he doesn't let you forget it". If you don't respond, it will be "*Such* a dull young man. He's been to all these *marvellous* places, and he literally hasn't got a *word* to say about them". Only great skill and much luck can save the social reputation of the Returned Traveller.

The position of the Returned Traveller is always delicate and frequently false. But things are ten times worse for him if he has been to some place more than ordinarily remote and commonly reputed to be dangerous. This, as it happened, was the case with me. The perils I had met with were no greater, and indeed considerably less, than those to be encountered in any London street during the rush hour. But the place I had visited had so vile a name, its dangers had been presented so melodramatically to an expectant public by travellers more impressionable or more imaginative than myself, that my own mild and reassuring accounts of it would hardly carry instant conviction. Here again the Returned Traveller was in a nasty predicament; for the danger of being thought a woeful bore was hardly greater than the danger of being thought a would-be hero. To exaggerate—to pile on just enough of the agony to satisfy the lurid preconceptions of his hearers— would play too much havoc with his self-respect. But to tell the truth would be to incur suspicions of employing a particularly subtle form of braggadocio. This fellow (people would think), when he says that he found the climate delightful, the discomforts negligible, and the supposedly hostile natives much maligned, aims at establishing for himself a reputation for modest, unassuming heroism. No doubt he had little enough to put up with; but it cannot be as little as he says. It is easy enough to see that he is suppressing something; he hopes that we shall think he is suppressing a great deal.

At the thought of all this I groaned. A fan-shaped volley of flying fish scudded out from underneath the ship, bright, aspiring, ill-co-ordinated and ephemeral, like good resolutions. They disappeared, several at a time, into the flanks of the small waves: till at last only three, and then two, and then one was left, miraculously preserving his trajectory, to go skipping away from us towards the unattainable horizon....

When in the end he disappeared, I wondered if he too was called upon to play the Returned Traveller: was encouraged to dilate on his experiences in that element to which he had paid a more than ordinarily protracted visit: was implored by large smooth white fish, with ugly mouths and protruding eyes, to Tell Them All About The Air: was invited by primmer, altogether more beady fish to come down and give their shoal a talk next term: was asked, by decorative inane fish with a tendency to wriggle, whether he wouldn't be going off somewhere else directly, and didn't the sea seem too dreadfully boring after all his thrilling adventures in the air: was cross-examined by sage portentous public-spirited fish about the Standard of Living up there, and the rainfall, and what sort of chance a decent young fish with a public school education but practically no capital would have in this element whose potentialities were said to be so vast.... Poor little flying fish! My heart went out to him.

You must not think that I have overstated the horrors of being a Returned Traveller. Now I come to think of it, indeed, it has been the other way about. I see that I have handled his case too subjectively. Thus far, he appears from my diagnosis to be his own worst enemy: a hypersensitive creature, tortured by qualms too nice to be of general application, too finicky and eager in his fears. You may object that anyone so scrupulous to renounce a spurious prestige, anyone so morbidly analytical of his own capacity to bore, does not have to go round the world to put himself in a position which he finds distressing; he would have misgivings anywhere.

In this there is some shadow of the truth. But wait. I have dealt as yet with only a moiety of the afflictions which were to beset me in three weeks' time. Good fortune and address may do something to alleviate those largely private and internal tortures which I have described above. But nothing—not all the luck and all the skill in the world—can save or avert some of the perils to which he is exposed.

Nothing, for instance, can save the Returned Traveller from that woman who, catching sight of him across a crowded room shortly after he has come back from New Guinea, trumpets out in a ghoulish and acquisitive voice, "Ah, there is my dear So and So, just back from doing all those wonderful things in Alaska", and forthwith makes for you, collecting as she goes a whole reluctant echelon of your fellow-guests, and half-pushing, half-pulling them towards you, like a snow plough: all the while babbling with terrible distinctness, "Come and let's get him to tell us *all* about Alaska". So that in only about eight times as much time as it takes to tell you are at bay before a ring of curious and hostile faces, the owners of which have it on the best authority that you are going to give them the lowdown on Alaska.

It ought to be an easy situation to carry off. It ought to be simply a question of saying, in a firm but tactful voice, "As a matter of fact, it wasn't Alaska, it was New Guinea. The names are so very much alike, I always think, don't you?" perhaps adding, if you are in a charitable mood and want to save this frightful woman's frightful face, some little anecdote about how a lot of your luggage did actually go to Alaska by mistake, owing to your not having written the labels in block capitals. Yes, it ought to be an easy situation to carry off.

But somehow it never is. At least, I never find it so. I bungle the business of enlightening my inquisitors. Unnerved by the lust for information which smoulders in their eyes, I lose my head and miss my opportunity. I stammer. I smile apologetically. I omit altogether to correct the impression that I have just been to Alaska.

And now it is too late to do so. One of the leaders of the pack has given tongue: a steely-eyed and formidable woman,

who looks as if she reviews travel-books for a highbrow weekly
on the strength of a walking tour in Finland.

The cold, she supposes, was intense?

"No", I say weakly. "At least, not where I was."

After that I am done for. An M.F.H. cross-questions me
about the management of dog-teams. A man who once went
to Murren enquires knowingly about snow conditions. From
all sides there are cries of, "Let me see now, Alaska *is* in the
Empire, isn't it?" and "I wonder if you heard anything of a
young cousin of my wife's who went out there in '28", and
"The lichens are marvellous, they tell me". I have become,
for all practical purposes, a man who has just been to Alaska.
Protest is as useless as if I had been turned into a toad. The
cruel transformation is complete.

From this intolerably false position escape is only possible
by a ruse. It needs a more ruthless assurance than I can command to tell these people that they are barking up the wrong
hemisphere. It is too late now to say, "As a matter of fact, it
was New Guinea"; or at least one cannot say it without feeling an awful fool. One has become, however involuntarily, an
impostor; and one hardly likes to expose oneself.

In my experience, the only way out of this dilemma is to
pretend that you are either snow-deaf or snow-dumb, or perhaps
both, and therefore in no position to answer questions about
Alaska. After that you must leave the house with all possible
speed and hurry home to the *Encyclopaedia Britannica* (A–AUS).

And then there are the Experts. These constitute what is
virtually a Hidden Peril, owing to their protective colouring.
You would never spot them as a menace, these dim grey men
with pince-nez, who put questions to you in a soft and de-
precating voice. But what questions....

You have been holding forth, under compulsion, to an
audience which appears to be more than ordinarily ill-
informed and impressionable. Your tales have gone down
rather well. When you stop talking there is the usual ex-
clamatory salvo of polite appreciation.

Its echoes have hardly died away when you realise that an inoffensive, rather harassed little man sitting on the most uncomfortable chair in the room is addressing you. His voice is gentle yet compelling. Everyone listens to him.

"You must have had a good deal of trouble", he is saying, "with the *micaubas*?"

"With the what?"

"With the *micaubas*." His tone is ever so slightly reproachful.

"I don't think I ever——" you begin doubtfully.

"Oh, but you must have. That country's full of them. Why, in 1910 Squiffenhagen calculated that there were not less than 40 to every——"

Rashly, madly, hoping to regain by a long shot that prestige which is fast ebbing from you, you interrupt him; and thus sacrifice an important clue. For if you had only waited to hear what it was that, according to Squiffenhagen's calculations, carried, contained, or otherwise accommodated not less than 40 *micaubas*, you might at least be a step nearer to knowing whether a *micauba* was a fish, or a superstition, or an edible root, or a prevailing wind. As it is, you risk everything; and lose.

"Oh, *micaubas*!" you cry (pronouncing the word differently from the way he pronounces it). "You mean the water-earwigs, don't you? We always called them *scrujis*: the Indian name, you know."

"No, no, no", says the little man impatiently; all the apology has left his voice now. "Not Bostock's *Forficula aquatica*. Of course I don't mean those little fellows. I mean the big *micaubas*—the poisonous tree-frogs. You must have seen dozens of them."

"I don't remember——" You go through the motions of racking your brains. *Were* there any tree-frogs?

"Oh, come, come", says the little man, who has grown almost peremptory. "You surely don't mean to tell me——"

You are cornered. It is clear that the majority of those

present suspect you of being a charlatan, of never having gone
to these places at all. They eye the Expert with considerable
respect; they eye you with scorn and distrust. In self-defence
you take to dishonesty.

"Of course", you say, rather too hastily, "we *saw* plenty
of the little beggars; but they never gave us any trouble.
Squiffenhagen was always a bit of an alarmist, wasn't he?"
You utter what is intended for an airy laugh.

But it is no good. It is too late. They have seen through
you.

"*Do* tell us about the poisonous tree-frogs", says someone.
But she says it to the little man, to the Expert.

But in the end I suppose it is true that the Returned
Traveller is his own worst enemy. He has seen and done
things which have for him considerable significance, and he
is at first desperately anxious to communicate his experiences
to others. But when he tries to do this he finds that it is impossible. He is like a poet in a world where poetry is not
recognised as a form of expression. He has no medium in
which to work.

For it is not enough to tell the truth. The facts—the things
that happened—reproduce only a stiff and stunted image of
reality. The truth alone cannot recapture and project that
reality, any more than his camera has succeeded in im-
mortalising its subjects. His camera has reduced a wide river
at dawn to a blurred geometrical design, the magic detail of
the jungle to a scribble of tiresome intricacy. The truth will
do the same by his experiences.

How to convey the ecstasy of finding that river in a moment
of despair, at nightfall? "Well, you see, we were frightfully
thirsty. (Oh, and I forgot to tell you that the men had broken
one of the gourds against a tree, so we only had about a pint
of water left.) We kept on thinking of iced lager. It didn't
look as if we had a chance of finding the river that night....
And then suddenly someone shouted, and there was the river,

really a very beautiful river, and we rushed down and lay in
it and let it run down our throats: I simply can't describe to
you how good it felt, just to lie in it like that...."

"Yes," they will say, "that *must* have been a relief."

("*...and when we got to the station, they told us the train didn't
go till 5.50: so Henry had been right all the time—it wasn't the
5.40 after all——*"

"*Yes,*" *they will say,* "*that* MUST *have been a relief——*")

And so one will fail every time, largely through one's own
fault. And gradually one's memories will become shop-soiled
and unrecognisable, will take on some of the artificiality of
the markets in which they have been hawked. Every now and
then the true image of some incident will burst unexpectedly
through the stale, mechanical, unfelt phrases in which one is
clothing it for the hundredth time; and you will be appalled
to see how you have betrayed reality. A sound, a smell, an
inflection in someone's voice will recall all the detail and all
the significance of a scene; you will remember suddenly
exactly how it felt to live through that scene. And over against
that sudden memory of the truth stands the picture you are
drawing, a colourless travesty, a thing made wearisome and
false by repetition. From boring and deceiving others you
have come to bore and deceive yourself; for you, as well as
for your hearers, your experiences are second-hand. They
happened once; but they have been told many times. The
truth and meaning have gone out of them in the telling. They
are no longer even reflections; they are shadows.

The Portuguese ventriloquist had stopped. He was engaged in conversation with the Second Officer. The Second
Officer was telling him that we were just now crossing the
Equator. Both men looked over the side of the ship with a
gratified and rather expectant air, as if they had some hope
of seeing the Equator.

But the blue sea only gleamed in a desultory, unresponsive

way, and continued to hiss luxuriously under the hot, quivering boat. There was no sign of the Equator. But the imaginations of geographers had somehow trumped up an incident to break the monotony of our days; and we were indefinably reassured by contact with something so important, so official, so symmetrical.

One of my fellow-passengers came and leant over the rail beside me.

"Well," he said, in a lusty sort of voice, "back on the jolly old Equator!"

"Back?" I said.

"Yes. I lived on the Equator for seven years, in North Borneo. My bungalow was slap on top of it. I slept in one hemisphere and had breakfast in the other. At least that was what I always used to say." (And indeed it was easy to see that he had said it many times before.) "Funny thing, living on the Equator."

"You must tell me about it", I said dutifully. I was conscious of a dreadful sinking feeling: just such a feeling, I reflected, as I shall be arousing among my friends three weeks from now.

The Returned Traveller looked delighted.

"Of course", he began, "I'm not much of a hand at telling stories...."

During the next three weeks he spoke no truer words than those.

FALL IN, GHOSTS

"*Alonzo.* Captain!
  Martino. I am glad to see
Your valiant hand, and yours; but pray you, take notice,
My title's changed, I am a colonel.
  Pisano. A colonel! where's your regiment?
  Martino. Not raised yet;
All the old ones are cashier'd, and we are now
To have a new militia: all is peace here,
Yet I hold my title still, as many do
That never saw an enemy."
           —Massinger's *Bashful Lover*.

THE battalion had halted in the light shade of the line of poplars, which began to look a little unkempt aloft. Rifles had been piled into the usual little pyramids, men had seated themselves on their heavy packs, except the cooks and others with immediate duties. The cooks had lost no time. Their fires already breathed blue spires of smoke into the calm but subtle sky. Beneath that sky, two empires were at war. One village farther to the east, and you would have seen the furrowings and burnings of that dismay on the face of the land. Here there was not such obvious evidence. The big grey house with deep white window-sills at the turn of the field path, the farm with its square-set sheds and stalls among other poplars, the crucifix surmounting the steps of granite in the middle of the rootfields, the clean causeway, the trickling land-drain under the culvert did not report the imminence of an enemy. On a closer inspection, it would have occurred to you that some Rembrandtesque cabins among close canopies of apple-boughs, low brown cabins unbrightened with the spirit of the green season, must be the homes of guns. Those new ditches, with their hurdled sides, leading to circular workings and mounds of whitening earth and mazy wire fences, were nothing agricultural. The group of cottages at the cross-road a few hundred yards off had not, certainly, been attacked by a common fire; their beams and laths were

indeed a little blackened, but something had juggled them
into a wild series of angles against the daylight.

"What the deuce are you sitting here for, young man, and
watching your cooks make all this smoke? Get round and
stop them." The youth looked up at his friendly tyrant,
jumped to his feet and said, "I'm sorry, sir, I was told that the
men must have tea, and——" "Yes, that's right, but for
heaven's sake tell those fellows to keep their smoke under.
We're only two miles here from the German line." The youth
scurried away to the problem of preventing that smoke-
column from the cookers; which solved itself. Tea was up;
dixies were on the way round the leaning and laughing and
contemplating and dozing company. There was no need for
more smoke. He returned to the little group of officers, and
accepted his mug of tea without apprehension. The Major
had puzzled him afresh by his blend of correctiveness and
sympathy. The officers there—Green with his pipe and map,
Stephenson with his back against Green's—were commenting
on the place chosen for the halt, and the prospect of an aeroplane's catching sight of the whole move.

"Packs on!" The interval was over; the quiet morning
had failed to conjure up any burst of horror. The motor-
cyclist from Brigade had come and gone in bumping progress,
delivering the orders; and now the battalion was moving with
the most stylish ease it could along the cambered, cobblestone
Rue d'Aubépine. The hamlet with its shells of houses and its
beds and mattresses dangling over its crooked walls—does so
little plaster, and so little timber, and a front door and a
bureau make a dwelling?—was left behind. "You may
smoke." With rifles slung over their shoulders, the men were
in good mood. Songs sprang up, grew loud, and rival songs
intervened; you hardly knew which choir to join. "Who were
you *with* last night?" "England was England..."? Heads
moved left and right as interest arose with the approach to
common life. Civilians were met; one respectable French-
man had such a fierce goatee moustache that the battalion

with one accord, in the purest spirit of *entente cordiale*, set up a magnificent "Maa-aa". "See that, Nobby, that's an Estaminet. Where the M.M.P.'s stop." "O, a Rest-a-minute. Well, I'm willing." "This Country was made for war, sir. All these places were built to be knocked over easy. When did you see a shanty like that in England?"

"Appree la Guer fee*nee*."

"There was a fellow in the lot that relieved us, sir, who'd been in the secret service." "Why, that's odd; they say there's a fellow in this division whom the Germans are after and who's only safe up the line." "Well, perhaps that's the same man: He said von Krupp's hands were all going on strike this year." "Arthur, you're an optimist." "What did you call me?" "The first seven years will be the worst." "These Alleymans never wanted war you bet." "Why don't the Pope stop it?" "Ah, he's a Roman Catholic. Jerry's Protestant." "Ah." "Old Captain Rattle's beginning to sweat, look!—No, but why can't Freemasonry stop it?" "ESSARS two kilos; bet you we're in the line again to-night." "What? Not going *this* road. They say we're off to guard iron rations at le Havre." "Well, every time there's anything on the poor old Ninth click. Hi, there's old Sergeant Nell. Hey hey, Sergeant, how's the rum, how's the wife and family?— What, don't you remember him? He's been on some claims stunt since we was at Barnham Barracks. Nice job, with that bike. But they don't turn *him* out at eight." "March to attention!" At the entrance to another village, on the bank, there is the galaxy of command and authority which they know as a considerable element in their war. The General has a glittering eye above that collation of ribbons.

In such circumstances, many made their true discovery of the battalion, the large family, to which they had come as not very confident strangers. Good fortune and a few months improved the matter, you recollect, beyond all dreams. There had never been mutual understanding like it in your experience. Wherever you went, you saw a friend; if you drifted

into the quartermaster's stores out of the line, there was this
lively pleasure of welcome and acceptance; if you called to
the snipers in their lair in the saphead, there would be a
cheerful response, the sackcloth that hung behind them and
their promptly closed loophole would be drawn aside to
admit you, and you sat with them and their telescope in the
knowledge that they were glad. Every face and every name
was intensely known to you, while that life lasted. You grew
to judge men either as desirable or undesirable additions to
the family; the young pioneer officer, for example, with the
sly quiet epigrams and the unhurrying, entire control of a
strung-out party of spadesmen, never seemed to belong to his
own unit; he was yours by rights. The brilliantly invincible
transport officer of the next battalion, who seemed to turn up
anywhere—a shell exploded, and there *he* stood, with his latest
irony to tell you—was a part of your transport officer's
existence, and one implied the other. Some faces seemed
destined to go on for ever, for a battalion could not be suffered by whatever powers then ruled the mad hour to be
quite extinguished or supplanted. In them was concentrated,
after the frightful desolations of battle upon battle, the beauty,
faith, hope which flowered in the word, "the battalion". Or
was this an illusion? Very few men lived through the full
career of any unit (that perhaps is the more scientific term);
and, as those familiar faces became more remote, others became the typical, life-giving and sustaining presences with—
was it the same battalion? It had the same number and place
in the line. It was thought the same; but, perhaps, each of
us knew a battalion not quite identical with any other man's,
though we served long enough together and borrowed one
another's army correspondence-books for months and months.
Here before me is such a book, a legacy from one with whom
I have lain in chilly weeds ahead of our line, have walked and
talked in the cathedral of St Omer, have waited in our den of
a company headquarters for the downward crash of day-
break's secret. If any two ever shared a battalion as an un-

mistakable spiritual and corporal estate, he and I were the two. But what does his book tell me?

It says, I fancy, that there came a time when, long before I was struck off the strength, as they called it, before I ceased to help the permanent Fred Worley to screw in the long wire-pickets on dark nights, *my* battalion was a conception of the past. How fast the war had used up the burnt-offerings! Possibly the battle of the Somme, which had almost entirely transformed the roll of officers serving with us, had at once matured and written the epitaph for my conception; if not that, then the opening of the savage squalid battle for Passchendaele had marked the conclusion of that honourable love. Is it so even in normal life, in that kaleidoscope which goes by the name of Peace? I begin to conjecture it. Your world, or mine—would you claim continuity for the references of the term? Turning over my friend's book of the autumn of 1917, I do not find the name of one who had been, to him and to me, the first and last reverence as often as we repeated the word, "the battalion". He was gone. His successor, beloved by him, schooled by him, alert in his ideals, was with us, as he had been throughout; for the transition to a certain home-lessness of mood, the fault was not his. War like a cataract had swept the battalion away, was doing the same for the battalion that had still formed itself up; I do not know most of these names, though I must have seen the men. This carbon copy of a letter addressed (I believe) to me is as though I were reading lists of the wounded at Fontenoy or Malplaquet:

3 a.m. Gas shell bombardment still in progress though shelling slight. Casualties as under to above hour.

15767	Cpl. Johnson, V. H.	Wounded
15193	Pte. Sendall, C.	,,
8420	,, Gilbert, S.	,,
15171	,, Partridge, W.	Gassed, died
5837	,, Huggett, G.	Gassed
	(Gas masks blown off in these cases.)	
1539	Pte. Henry, C.	Wounded
15199	,, Wilkinson	,,

Then there is the recommendation of 2271 Pte. Simmons, A. A., for the following action in an attack which I too was obliged to take part in—and for the past fifteen years I had never thought of this extraordinary youth as being in *my* battalion.

> Single-handed killed 4 enemy officers, sending in valuable information promptly early in the attack. Later took charge of night listening posts, two nights running, and was killed by a sniper by the Steenbeck.

What was he like, when did he join us, was he with V. that morning when V. and I laughed hysterically in the trenches just left by the Germans to us and the German barrage? Not a sound.

Did the same obliterative effect happen to you, do you think it would have done? If "household gods plant a terrible fixed foot", so do some associations; they have a hatred for anything like superannuation and substitutes. In that dizzy period of dreams, rumours, upheavals, fears, escapades, vanities, immeasurable moments, apprehensions, that which one had gained as a sheltering, steady, warm abiding-place in nature became especially precious. At one time it was actual, present, daily and hourly—and when that date was expired, among the other dreams this dream stood long, the shadow of a great rock in that weary land. The odd thing is, I suppose, that a number of us, who are no very enthusiastic metaphysicians, still cling to our rock; and, without noticing what we are doing, we submerge our individual differences of experience and choice, and the horribly rapid mutations of the war history of an infantry force as a human group. We come together, once a year, without allusion to the details of our own former shares of the history that concerns us, and we reanimate—the battalion. It is our quaint attempt at catching a falling star.

In my opinion we do it very tolerably. We have—at present—more qualifications than might have been expected. At one of our evenings, this fact was expressed with abrupt emotion by one of us who had been "in foreign parts" and had only just heard in time that there was a regular reunion of our camp. "Gentlemen," he began, "I am glad to be here; it is surprising to see that so many of us are alive. No ghosts here? nobody feeling a little out of his element?" And, I thought, some of the diners glanced round the room as if they half felt one or two figures, thus challenged, would "make themselves air". This proving to be mere fancy, we may indeed remark with restrained applause that a number of those who were famous for their being so largely the battalion are in the land of the living yet. There is G. H. H., to begin with; and we could almost eat him, but a divinity round our Colonel prevents the instinctive cannibalism from doing what it would. "Doesn't look a day older", whispers sergeant to sergeant—no, Mr Davey, D.C.M. to Mr Worley, D.C.M.— as G. H. H. rises to address us, and confesses that when he received orders to quit his original Regiment and come to us, above all when he first saw us, he was filled with wrath and— "well, I won't tell you what I did think", with a twinkling eye. He then tells us how he grew to delight in commanding us—and a (still sober) voice fills a pause, "And you weren't. . . so bad". Memories of the Somme will follow, and, as G. H. H. is a soldier by descent and character, when he has blessed us for sitting so patiently in the mudholes of the Schwaben Redoubt he blesses us even more vividly for marching in to Doullens, singing our song, not a "column of lumps" but— the battalion. What makes the appearance of G. H. H. among us so completely appropriate and remindful is the fact that on his right, with his mallet of office in his hand, sits J. L., his adjutant, our wisest, heartiest, safest guide—under G. H. H. —now as in 1916. When J. L. speaks, hesitation, melancholy, dispute are impossible; good sense and manhood seem our natural and inseparable qualities. He, too, appears to us very little altered from the days when, watching all and worrying none, he rode his horse over the training-ground behind Arras, or when he sat in that stifling glum cave

beyond Hamel with the Colonel, ignoring the blasts of high
explosive at the gaping entrance, trying to hold a crazy
attack in its proper place.

We have C.M. too, and who could fail to recognise him
still, at the other end of the hall? He was an integral part of
my battalion which, as I confessed, slipped away from me.
I recall the admiration I felt at his mighty throwing of bombs,
and his going ahead of us to Thiepval when that poor place
was still being gunned and bombed and bayonetted and
gassed for the lease. He has a spirit which I envy, for, in part
freeing himself from this incubus-like inspiration of ours, he
studies what men were before the calamity, and what they
now are and under what conditions. His speech is not over-
reminiscent, but gay, comfortable, a little risky. He, indeed,
makes us a little uneasy about our recurrence to the bitter
past, the rhapsodical touch in our reason for being here. Are
we becoming romantic? G.M. here is not; he always was.
Rosy youth never deserted him, with all its glowing sensi-
bilities. He dramatised, or enjoyed the dramatic in, the
dreariest situations of the grey old confusion. He was one of
the few who would speak of God without the purposes of
exasperation, as a sublime, inscrutable and natural Being
even above the swilling mudpools of Spoil Bank. His finest
gesture we take to have been in the greasy but protective
tunnels of Canada Street—the one shelter between Gheluvelt
and Ypres then; having just performed a damnable miracle
in delivering certain supplies at a gas-filled and thunderous
spot called a Copse, he reported "completion" to the
General. The General turned from his plank table and
guttering candles, and, finding that G.M. had no receipt for
the supplies, became excited, harangued, sent him off to get
one in that ghoulish night. G.M. went, found another human
being at the Copse, obtained the receipt, returned to the
General, saluted in his finest manner as he submitted the
paper, and withdrawing in perfect silence saluted again.
And this fantasy or faith we find still when G.M. comes in

among us. He should do it on horseback! but his conversation is as blithe as that would be.

So far I have been speaking of those who were our officers —I have chosen one or two, from whose examples you are to understand the whole number; and that I do so and accord them precedency is not forced. It is in the order of our reunion. The "other ranks", the "N.C.O.'s and men", at least on such occasions preserve their battalion's spirit as they knew it, not unceremoniously; their officers must be officers still, men of trust, commissioned after all by the King, honourable and fine. I have seen many varieties of beautiful simplicity in this life. The ancient Japanese farmer, making me at home on his rough and ready *tatami*, a trifle hard up for topics, suddenly remembered a means of coming nearer: what a smile of delight he had when he said, "your country and mine were allies in the War, weren't they?" The childless wife, talking softly to the nesting blackbird that knew her, was a picture of beauty. With such treasures I count the voluntary, sweet and accomplished courtesy which I see in our reunions from the men to the officers—and from them again, in another and equally valuable sense, to the men.

How, one asks again, did some of these "other ranks" come through? C.A.U., for example, without whom half of us perhaps might not have heard of these evenings, went through fire and water indescribable; not only has he come through, he is radiant with a mastery of life. This is the kind of man who is jostled in the street by many who would have fallen to pieces with a tithe of his burdens in Flanders; the fact never occurs to him, and he would think it not worth the note of indignation. Order and cheerfulness go where he goes, the rations are served out, the complainants treated to a quick epigram on their size in jaws, stomachs and opinions, and he is visiting the listening-posts in the rat-haunted crater. With him is quiet J.C., whom nobody ever offended or felt a wish to offend—his fortunate company depended on his thoughtful unerring work for years. A.D. and F.W. are

together—that friendship was famous! Their shyness has not
passed away; perhaps it has even increased. Of these two
men, too much was demanded; have I not been guilty of that
myself, not noticing that even they could feel the last straw?
W. A. C. comes over to give a hint or two for the speeches.
I doubt whether he slept on the average three hours a day
and night in 1916 and 1917. I remember his pale face (I
wished a great painter might have seen him as I did) when,
in a dead midnight, he looked up from the mass of papers by
which the battalion partly retained its right to exist. A mystic
might have had that look; and I can interpret—C. had for
the battalion that kind of constant perceiving love which de-
nies all self-concern. Once he and I had a swamp to cross,
tree-stump by tree-stump; our predecessors there were there
still—very still—for there was a ferocious shelling on it. He
was laughing to me as we set out—and here we are, and he is
attributing what I praise in him to "mainly Memory"—the
calm ambiguous rogue!—and saying, "I can give you some
stories about Avard". Now T. Y. ventures to claim a word;
him too I remember mainly at night, with the signallers'
headphones on, doing his best with the squeaky buzzer, going
on for ever if need be. That loud and frequent cry "Basso"
sounds across our talk and the noise of the assembly; Basso is
used to it; he is a hospitable humorist, apparently unaltered
since the Western Front. When it comes, as it must, to my
making a speech, you will see one listener particularly
anxious and, if we have luck, particularly applauding, from
the far end of the room; that tall youth, with the shining
ruddy cheek and the golden hair. H. T. N. was a runner, and
few runners ever failed in their solitary courage; he excelled.
His friend, H., of his own calibre, should be here; H. T. N. is
just a shade disconsolate, but his smiling face can never be
darkened.

The rest of them? I could name many, and—here is that
old dilemma—many I could not. They came, probably, when
I began to be retrospective, in the very midst of our war

history, over the battalion; when the hurry, and hopelessness, and a new selfishness, reduced my powers of becoming acquainted. Now and then, they will overcome diffidence and give me a clue which leads back to a scene that had been concealed. It is a pity that S.J.S. is not here this evening; he is the infallible index to everyone, and everything—the walking log-book of the battalion. Yet for me, who am to address the party, it may be as well that he is prevented; one slip over a name or a date, and he "could throw a plate at you". But error is one thing, legend another. I find in some of us an innocent formation of legends in process—a natural outgrowth from our longing to keep in view the battalion we served with as, in its way, "a glorious birth". G.H.H. himself ascribes to me, and has described to the assembled host, a far from attractive patrol in the marshes east of Hamel Mill; he asseverates—no slighter term will do—that I announced to him my intention of the patrol and of writing a poem on the Mill, and that I accomplished both. Possibly I told him of the patrol afterwards with poetic licence; at all events, he is as sure of it as of the poem, which I actually produced to him. Then, my dear E.F., to whom I owed many of my first sensible movements in the region of Festubert and La Bassée Canal, has been pressing me to agree with his reminiscences of an adventure, on the night when Beaumont Hamel was being taken (be grateful, you absentees!), which betrayed young Johnson and myself a long way into the German zone. How approvingly should I have seen E.F. with us; but, though he declares he was, and that it was he who repeatedly informed me that we were well on the way to Berlin, I am telling you— not him—that he was not. He joined us afterwards, at the south-east corner of Thiepval Wood; and had the high-velocity shells fallen a few yards otherwise just then there would have been no chance of my thus asserting the grace of accurate history. But am I right? Is it grace? I grow shadowy myself, and next year I shall be liable to substantiate E.F.'s projections in every letter.

These oddities I mention as being within my own area; but the evening advances, the speeches and the music are drawing to an end—all but my speech, which J. L. has placed last on the bill. He replies, to my protest, that at that stage nobody will take any notice of what is actually said; the battalion is not teetotal yet; the beer is not the "bière speciale pour Cantines" which we inhaled at Poperinghe. Many seats, in front of the tables decorated with our blue and orange colours, are empty now, and their occupants are heartily exchanging recollections and liquids at the business side of the restaurant. Tankards and tumblers are gently set down before us, and—may I boast of it unblamed?—a hand or two ruffles my hair, a voice or two says "Don't you wish it was the old Eleventh?" and "There my dear, you're a good old boy". The old Eleventh! I shall be speaking to them— to these who would, at need, give up everything this hour to follow G. H. H. again in some rare enterprise, even to be "crimed" by G. M. for dirty harness and led by me into some absurd predicament; but not only to them. Were I a maker of tragic spectacle, I could fill some of those vacated seats with forms as piteous as Banquo's. There is no need for that, no need for vacant places; those to whom I would also be audible, and by whose judgment I am content to stand or fall, are present to most of our minds. The great Essayist who declined, even in his illustrious Elian wit-melancholy, to put himself on paper, once called on his schoolfellow Coleridge to re-possess his vision: "Come back into memory, like as thou wert in the dayspring of thy fancies". We could use the phrase, and the feeling is ours; for we have never permitted ourselves to think of our best men as the mangled victims of the vile machinery that ended their toil. They come back alive, hale, genial, ready to be anything in the hope of being ever.

Come, Daniels. G. H. H. was at one time inclined to be your severe critic. He "has heard more since", and you know how he loved you after all. Here is Worley—you remember how you discovered in him the original of Bairnsfather's "Old Bill". Had I but dreamed you would soon be—but you were always a humanist. There are no bags of Very Lights now for you to send up to the company headquarters, no parade states; be free. If you will, we will be on parade at six; but now relax, and see around you what you were to us. And Ashford, you are not likely to be far off on such a night. There is no champagne going—you have forgotten? I haven't; it was you who introduced me in your best manner to that wine. It was one summer evening, dusky-brilliant, and I was emerging from a talk about next day's training programme with C. in his office, in the labourer's cottage at Houlle. Moulle! Houlle. Ah, well,

> How delightfully we would go
> To Houlle and Moulle
> And the bathing-pool
> And the—

Preparations for the show? But, about that Heidsieck, I was emerging, it was hard to see for a moment, and there was a voice, your voice, and a hand, your hand, and a bottle, your bottle; and on the whole I liked champagne. Next morning I said I didn't? But there were later tests. I wish you would tell me—did you ever feel fear? I never noticed it. I saw you melancholy once, without a smile—it was when I came to say I was for England. You had a prescient gift, I thought, and not only then. This is Clifford. Easiest of friendships, ours; how imperceptibly we drew together, until if I was on the duckboards towards Hill 60 I could be pretty sure the man following me was you. We hardly had our fair share of walks and gossip in peaceful places—I see you almost inevitably with a slab of muddy sandbags behind you, and your telescope under your arm. You even recall my giving you my field-glasses? Well, you were very flattering about them, and then, you did something with them. It all sounds dreamy now, absurd almost; how your eyes shone as you described the German trolley-pushing party that you were observing

towards Comines! You would not have changed places then
with Rockefeller, I think you said. Calm as a country Sunday
you moved through your last labours. Blue-eyed and fair,
reasonable and—but it is no courtesy to praise a man to his
face. Anyway, put those field-glasses under the table. Tice!
our own Prussian! The Prussians are not now regarded as
they were, journalistically, when you were in the dugout on
Canal Bank. No, my dear, we did not *mean* that you were a
caricature Prussian in grain! I am ashamed to have lost the
address of that excellent widow-woman near Zuytpeene who
was so proud of having so gentle, so wise, so saintly a being
under her roof as Tice; and what a dinner she put up for us,
your friends. I liked the letter she wrote you better than the
Story of Ruth; I wrote to her after July 31st. If I think of
Clifford with a pair of binoculars, I think of you with a map-
case and a compass; throw them away, you old non-sleeper,
and listen to what Collyer there is saying. He is surely not
talking of Pozières? He is, and, thanks to our army training,
we know he is although he refers to it as Jammy Whiskers.
Vidler interrupts with a tale he heard in Vancouver, no, it is
simply his imitation of a Chinese laundry-boy, followed by—
O Vid, we know it by heart, *par cœur*, well, "It's like this here,
sir, not feeling quite meself this morning, sir, I eats all right
and I sleeps all right, but——"

At our last feast, there was one with us whom we could not
imagine ever being away. He is away, this year, and except
under the dispensation which has just permitted me to fill up
some of the empty chairs with my lost companions, he will
be away throughout the series now. Regimental Sergeant-
Major Ball was what is called a "character", and a little
perturbed and suspicious about his being regarded as such.
Perhaps that was the only reason why he was now and then
subdued. But what should he do about it? After all—and
then he would release the full benefit of his personality and
colloquial zest. With a short explosion of a laugh he would
drive home his point. "And you remember them fellows I

brought in out of No Man's Land, and brought into that water-store where you was? And you remember how blasted dry we all were and so were you, and there didn't seem to be anything for it except drink that water? But—there was something else. I hadn't got my water-bottle on for nothing, had I? You remember? IT CAME UP RUM!" Of course it did. Ball had a lusty spirit, a loud indignant geniality, which made anything less than rum impossible even in a smashed water-store on the edge of a murderous and groaning No Man's Land. A singer, too, at battalion gaffes. Once he "came on", at such a concert in a capital big hutment far from enemies, just after a turn by two mischievous young accomplices who had mimicked with deplorable accuracy the gestures and the conversation of — Ball. Either he had not quite detected that or he had decided to triumph by sheer and complete agreement and superior demonstration; for he strode the platform full of his grand manner—to say, I again suggest, that

> None but himself could be his parallel.

Eyeing the house as he would eye a squad of defaulters, he opened his mouth to give us a most monotonous ballad of which he produced the words with impressive emphasis—so much so, that after fifteen years I remember them, or some of them.

> Once I *went* to a Res-taw-*rong*
> With an appetite about *Twelve yards long*;
> Ordered poultry [here he shrugged his shoulders], up it *came*,
> When it got there, it was GAME;
> A sort of a *tarry twang* arose
> As soon as I touched it on the *nose*....
>> Postponed,
>> Me Dinner,
>>> &c.

As he sang, there grew an imperfectly repressed murmur of delight from front to back of the hall; Ball seemed aware of it, and, like the traveller in Mr de la Mare's haunted forest, he

expressed himself "even louder", and rolled on triumphantly
to the final stanza and its "Postponed—The Wedding".

Ball, in spite of the apparent impossibility, is dead and gone;
I mentioned his occasionally lapsing into a subdued manner.
Now, for all the jubilation, commotion, talk, speechifying and
chorusing in the room to-night, a subdued manner may be
perceived in the individuals, and if we could investigate it
without these agreeable interruptions (signing menus on these
occasions has to be done, in Keats's words, with "a fine
excess") we might again discover "the battalion". On the
whole, as G.H.H. remarked with such parental pleasure, the
Peace has not treated our lucky lads too harshly in matters of
common prosperity; they seem, most of them, to be holding
their own with necessity, even if we allow that some absentees
were kept away by poverty. Not thence comes the subdued
manner. But, if I may diagnose, these are for ever a shade
different from those who missed their former experiences.
They are accustomed to looking into those memories which
would not often be welcome talk to their neighbours. They
see the works of the Lord, but His wonders in the deep are
past; those too they saw. The mystery of that, the misery and
the dignity reside for them in the word, "the battalion". The
future cannot rival that attraction. They, we, are years behind
even the present, and minor reservations and limitations of
date, place and contact yield to one strong retrospective
migratory devotion. But J.L. is hammering again to warn us
of a speech, and I am the machine that must make it. I am
less sure of my past and present than I pretended to be when
we sat down. Will there be chairs enough for all of us, as the
troops return to the tables to listen forgivingly to this rhetoric?
At what point do we separate from those other listeners I
named? Are we not all in the same boat? Fall in, ghosts.

Note. The preceding impression is actually derived from an annual dinner attended not by one battalion, but by three, which were raised and brigaded together and shared the same career in France and Belgium. For my purpose I have only alluded to members of my own unit, with hardly an exception; were I writing at greater length, this would not have been the case; but my purpose was to typify. This explanation is due to my friends of the 12th and 13th battalions, if any of them should chance to see my essay; their part in the whole is not excluded for any reason but that of the simplicity demanded by my writing limits.